No Time to Retreat

No Time to Retreat
Why We Must Solidify Multicultural Education

By

Festus E. Obiakor
Sunny Educational Consulting, USA

United Kingdom – North America – Japan
India – Malaysia – China

Emerald Publishing Limited
Emerald Publishing, Floor 5, Northspring, 21-23 Wellington Street, Leeds LS1 4DL

First edition 2025

Copyright © 2025 by Emerald Publishing Limited.
All rights of reproduction in any form reserved.

Cover photo: iStock and Rawpixel

Reprints and permissions service
Contact: www.copyright.com

No part of this book may be reproduced, stored in a retrieval system, transmitted in any form or by any means electronic, mechanical, photocopying, recording or otherwise without either the prior written permission of the publisher or a licence permitting restricted copying issued in the UK by The Copyright Licensing Agency and in the USA by The Copyright Clearance Center. Any opinions expressed in the chapters are those of the authors. Whilst Emerald makes every effort to ensure the quality and accuracy of its content, Emerald makes no representation implied or otherwise, as to the chapters' suitability and application and disclaims any warranties, express or implied, to their use.

British Library Cataloguing in Publication Data
A catalogue record for this book is available from the British Library

ISBN: 978-1-83708-903-1 (Print hardback)
ISBN: 978-1-83708-905-5 (Print paperback)
ISBN: 978-1-83708-902-4 and 978-1-83708-904-8 (Ebook)

Typeset by TNQ Tech
Cover design by TNQ Tech

CONTENTS

About the Author .... *vii*

Foreword by Dr. Sean Warner .... *ix*

Preface .... *xiii*

1. Why Multiculturalism Matters in Education and Life *1*

2. Why the Search for New Meaning Matters in Multicultural Education *13*

3. Why Good Dispositions Matter in Multicultural Interactions *19*

4. Why Spirituality Matters in Multicultural Education *29*

5. Why Diversity, Equity, and Inclusion Projects and Initiatives Matter in Education *37*

6. Why Valuing the Gifts and Talents of Multicultural Persons Matters in Education and Life *45*

7. Why Voices of Students From Culturally and Linguistically Diverse Backgrounds Matter in Education *55*

8. Why Voices of Families From Culturally and Linguistically Diverse Backgrounds Matter in Education *63*

9. Why Community Voices Matter in Multicultural Education and Interactions *69*

10. Why Good Leadership Matters in Multicultural Education and Advancements.. 77

11. Why the Comprehensive Support Model Matters in Multicultural Education and Interactions... 85

12. Why Global Education Matters in Multicultural Education and Interactions... 97

13. Why Advancing Multicultural Skills Matters in Life Journeys........ 105

Afterword: Multiculturalism and Beyond... 111

References 121

ABOUT THE AUTHOR

Festus E. Obiakor, PhD, is the Chief Executive Manager of Sunny Educational Consulting; and his graduate degrees are from Texas Christian University and New Mexico State University. Though he was born in Sapele, Delta State, Nigeria, he is traditionally and culturally from Obodoukwu (the birthplace of his father), Imo State, Nigeria. Before immigrating to the United States for graduate school, he taught at Niblick Grammar School, Oghada, Bendel State; Aiyetero-Iloro Grammar School, Iloro-Ekiti, Ondo State; Ekamefa Grammar School, Ilasa-Ekiti, Ondo State; Oba Girls Secondary School, Anambra State; and Iheme Memorial Secondary School, Arondizuogu, Imo State. In the United States, as a university Professor, he taught at New Mexico State University, Las Cruces, New Mexico; Rust College, Holly Springs, Mississippi; The University of Tennessee-Chattanooga, Tennessee; Henderson State University, Arkadelphia, Arkansas; Emporia State University, Emporia, Kansas; University of Wisconsin-Milwaukee, Wisconsin; The City College of New York, New York; and Valdosta State University, Valdosta, Georgia. And, he served as Department Chair/Head at both The City College of New York, City University of New York and Valdosta State University, respectively. A teacher, scholar, leader, and consultant, he has served as Distinguished Visiting Professor at a variety of universities. He is the author of more than 250 publications, including books, chapters, articles, and commentaries; and he has presented more than 300 papers at national and international conferences. He serves on the editorial boards of reputable nationally and internationally refereed journals, including *Multicultural Learning and Teaching* (*MLT*) in which he serves as Founding/Executive Editor.

FOREWORD

Sean Warner
Clark Atlanta University

For almost half a century, Dr. Festus E. Obiakor has been unrelenting in challenging sedentary parochial mindsets related to educating culturally and linguistically diverse (CLD) and vulnerable young people and supporting their families, particularly in the exceptional education space. He has continued to inspire and ignite the hearts and minds of teachers, researchers, practitioners, scholars, administrators, and politicians with his insights (read Obiakor, 2001, 2007, 2008, 2018, 2020, 2021, 2023). *No Time to Retreat: Why We Must Solidify Multicultural Education* serves as the full and complete exemplification of Obiakor's thinking about multiculturalism and reminds us of our humanity in a genuine and unfeigned way.

As someone who has served in all multidimensional educational roles, I can attest to the fact that Obiakor's body of work, especially this recent rendering, resonates with how I have interacted with myself and others. Being a foreign-born African American male, I negotiate a White supremacist cultural milieu that capriciously grants me access to things when it is convenient or when it fails to challenge racialized norms. And, as a former New York City college dropout who rose to the level of Dean, School/College of Education, twice, at two minority serving institutions of higher learning, Obiakor's work reaffirms my determination to make a difference in a world so similar but so complex. We are similar because we see ourselves in other people and want and need what they want and need; however, we are complex because we are all uniquely different intra-individually and inter-individually. I see myself as one of those with multidimensional ways of showing up in the world and as a human-being with gifts and assets often overlooked because of westernized conventions, adroitly supported by our institutions and systems, that tell us what and whom are worth our time and attention and what and whom are not.

Thinking back, growing up as a young foreign-born African American boy in Jamaica, Queens, New York, I went from college dropout to college Dean in a ten-year span. Obiakor's newest rendering, *No Time to Retreat* speaks squarely to my academic, professional and sociocultural journeys; and the journeys of many others who because of societal messaging questioned their value and worth. Like many college dropouts from immigrant families residing in the US, sometimes you wonder with the ultimate question, WHO CARES? This is when you contemplate all kinds of good, bad, and ugly thoughts. You find yourself in a perpetual state of negotiating the tensions associated with self-worth and self-efficacy as informed by immediate family members, first, and then by the rest of the world second. For me, I was forced to question how my initial understanding of the world and my place in it comports with or deviates from what I was experiencing. In reality, this dynamic rests at the center of all CLD peoples' realities. It is the main prism through which they make sense of critical decisions they need to make for themselves and their loved ones. It is a multidimensional, multifaceted, and most importantly a multicultural perspective that is instantaneously ever-morphing; and as such creating new worlds through which to navigate and negotiate. Unlike the privileged class, positionalities can and do shift. My thinking as a rising junior communications major in college was that I was not learning anything or sufficiently prepared to enter the multitude of career opportunities in the field of communications. And interestingly enough, like most poor first generation CLD college students, was already conditioned to treat bank loans like free candy and borrow beyond my foreseeable means. It was like a game that I was playing with myself wherein I was pretending to be an informed industrious collegian with clear aspirations of what came next in the way of a profession, but no real sensibility of the path ahead.

In this book, Obiakor reiterates the need to be aware of who we are and why it is necessary to shift paradigms and powers to solve personal and societal problems. We can only move forward when we recognize and solve our problems. Strangely enough, dropping out of college in my junior year was probably the best move that I ever made. It focused my attention and realigned my intention. I dropped out of my undergraduate program in 1988 and in the spring of 1998 graduated with my doctorate degree in education from a top-tier New England and world class institution. What changed? I identified my inherent gifts and talents and saw the world beyond what I and many others had been conditioned to see and strategically weaponized the multidimensionality of my cultural self to navigate the academy. The question remains, How do we make institutions and organizations to authentically respond to people like myself? In this book, Obiakor speaks directly to this dilemma. He explains and demonstrates how schools and other institutions historically characterize the social and cultural differences of multicultural persons as diminutive, infinitesimal, and unworthy when juxtaposed against the dominant Europeanized culture. Obiakor further substantiates, in this expressly diversity, equity, and inclusion (DEI) world, why it is imperative for institutions and organizations to structurally center CLD students. Anything less elaborately (a) communicates a lack of readiness and willingness to challenge normally abnormal racist norms; and (b) shows how committed they are to talking and faking instead of doing and delivering.

In the fall of 1988, I took my first job as a young faculty member at a predominantly White southern institution. It was a top 50 public institution and of course had a tremendous collegiate football program. The level of regular macroaggressions that I endured from staff, faculty, and students were like nothing I had ever encountered. It went from faculty questioning the legitimacy of my work to students treating me like a joke in class. In fact, in my first semester, a student made an off-handed joke about "lynching" in my class. Yes, lynching! Of course, I was jolted and shocked; however, I turned it into a teachable moment. What teacher-education program properly prepares one for such an encounter, particularly with students who are preparing to be teachers? Up until my arrival, there was no doubt that my mostly White students saw themselves as the standard for anything equated with normalcy. Before long, with my teaching and support, they began to realize, understand, and question this framing. In addition, they learned that culture and the social construct we call race are not synonymous and that they had been miseducated about themselves and persons from CLD backgrounds. Generally speaking, in my professional career as a teacher-educator, students who I have trained to become teachers are given opportunities to confront their views on reality—they consistently benefitted from challenging their original truths. Metaphorically, two plus two may not have been equal to four; and if that is true, what does this mean for how they make sense of the world? While they seemed to be sometimes uncomfortable, they consistently wrestled with new ideas and who they wanted to be as teachers. Are these not what teaching and growth are all about?

In this book, Obiakor asks us to be lovingly critical of forces, people, institutions, and governments that are vested in pushing back multimodal, multidimensional, and most importantly multicultural ways of knowing, seeing, hearing, and communicating. And, I agree with him! I believe we must take the same approach with ourselves, which in many ways requires more effort, more commitment, and more diligence. Given our current political and geopolitical climates, the message driven home by Obiakor in *No Time to Retreat* is that we urgently need voices of multicultural persons. These voices are critical to helping us find ways to improve, enhance, and uplift the human condition for all people. Finally, this book teaches us to be spiritually outfitted, sufficiently equipped, and up to the task to prick the collective consciousness in such a manner that positions us to reimagine robust equity-based frameworks that are devoid of talk and decoration. All of these will hopefully reignite our resolve to ensuring that spaces and chances are created for all voices and perspectives to participate in our democratic nation and our ever-changing world.

References

Obiakor, F. E. (2001). *It even happens in "good" schools: Responding to cultural diversity in today's classrooms.* Corwin Press.
Obiakor, F. E. (2007). *Multicultural special education: Culturally responsive teaching.* Pearson Merrill/ Prentice Hall.
Obiakor, F. E. (2008). *The eight-step approach to multicultural learning and teaching* (3rd ed.). Kendall/Hunt.
Obiakor, F. E. (2018). *Powerful multicultural essays for innovative educators and leaders: Optimizing "hearty" conversations.* Information Age.
Obiakor, F. E. (2020). *Valuing other voices: Discourses that matter in education, social justice, and multiculturalism.* Information Age.
Obiakor, F. E. (2021). *Multiculturalism still matters in education and society: Responding to changing times.* Information Age.
Obiakor, F. E. (2023). *Reducing hate through multicultural education and transformation.* Information Age.

PREFACE

Life's happiness and sadness are based on multidimensional situations that have multidimensional ramifications; and these ramifications are experientially and perceptually based. This means that our experiences influence our perceptions. Though these perceptions might be right or wrong, they are tied to our race, culture, language, national origin, religion, gender, and personal idiosyncrasy (Obiakor, 2001, 2007, 2018, 2021, 2023). But, for us to live, be educated, work, and interact harmoniously together, we must get out of our own narrow confines to look for ways to deal with others different from us. By looking for ways, we are inspired to value, learn, teach, modify, adjust, collaborate, consult, and cooperate. These are basically the reasons for multicultural education and human existence, the central themes of *No Time to Retreat: Why We Must Solidify Multicultural Education*. Books of this nature are necessary for this day and age; not because of their controversial takes, but because they help us to see better, hear better, think better, talk better, do better, and succeed better.

    Daily, we see people who shock us by rationalizing a lot, overthinking a lot, giving excuses a lot, refusing to think a lot, remaining angry a lot, and losing their minds a lot. As it stands, somehow somewhere, someone seems bothered by someone or something; and, something disheartening seems to happen somewhere to someone. For some reason, these happenings create noises that are becoming a part of our lives. Scared, worried, and anxious, we continue to move on! *No Time to Retreat* urges us to continuously move on, be true to form, and not quit. Many of the hullabaloos in the United States and the world today are scary enough to force people to quit. In some strange fashion, the "rich" and the "poor" appear equally angry. While the "rich" is angry that he/she is paying too much tax, the "poor" is angry that he/she is poor and no one cares. For example, to add to our anxiety, we now have a group that wants to "Make America Great Again" and another group that wants to "Save the Soul of America;" and, there are other such groups around us advocating for one reason or another. As it appears, grievances are becoming overwhelmingly out of control—they have led to what Frank Bruni (2024) called "the age of grievance." These convoluted divisive situations are taking over our placidity; and very few people seem to care or pay attention despite the dangers that they pose. The questions then are, Do we run away? Do we fight back? Do we give up? Or, do we find innovative solutions to move us forward? As a teacher-scholar and professional in education, I believe in finding and sharing innovative solutions to our endemic problems as I have done in this book.

One perennial issue that continues to linger around is whether or not multicultural education is needed, relevant, and useful. Some have argued that multicultural education is (a) a non-issue today because racism is over; and (b) divisive, controversial, and should not be talked about. However, others like me have argued that since it involves human-beings, it must be talked about and used as an enhancement tool for humanity. From my perspective, just the hyperbolic assumption that "racism is over" actually (a) is aggravating and symptomatic of how low and mentally uncurious we have stooped; and (b) makes the case for teaching, learning, and valuing human differences. *No Time to Retreat* challenges our assumptions and actions toward different "others" and inspires us to take multicultural education seriously even when it sounds and appears simplistic. While I believe the appearance of simplicity unfairly treats multicultural education as something that is personally and societally unimportant, everything about it affects our sacred existence as human-beings. In other words, as long as humanity exists, multicultural education will never cease to exist. This book recognizes this reality and prescribes transformational ways that interrogate our negative perceptions, judgments, and treatments of people who are different from us. In addition, it addresses ways to maximize the fullest potential of people from culturally and linguistically diverse (CLD) and vulnerable backgrounds. Typically, people from CLD backgrounds are systematically misidentified, misassessed, mislabeled/miscategorized, misplaced, and misinstructed. As a result, they are frequently disenfranchised, disadvantaged, disillusioned, and demeaned.

As a teacher-scholar, I believe we cannot teach what we do not know, play with people we hate or do not like, lead people we do not know, or work together with people we do not trust. We cannot continue to masquerade what everyone sees and knows—doing this creates possibilities that lead to fraudulent multiculturalism. *No Time to Retreat* reiterates why multicultural education matters in all aspects of life and why it is imperative that we continue to teach people about different "others." This book asserts that this is not the time to retreat and that this is the time to solidify multicultural education, especially if we are truly serious about reducing historic educational and societal problems of misidentifying, misassessing, mislabeling/miscategorizing, misplacing, and misinstructing CLD students, their families, and their communities (Obiakor, 2001, 2007, 2018, 2021, 2023). It is sad that some educational professionals endeavor to teach people to be good and perfect while they continue to be soulless and imperfect professionals. We must divorce ourselves from soullessness and continue to learn and teach innovatively as difficult as it may seem!

No Time to Retreat gives us a lot to think about—it urges us to use our spiritual lens to search for new meaning and supports our curiosity to wonder and think about new situations and solutions. It is important that we wonder why (a) colleagues and school leaders allow their fellow colleagues to negatively talk about CLD students and families in their faculty/staff lounges; (b) educators, community leaders, and government agencies are not bothered by the high rates of prejudicial suspension and expulsion of CLD and vulnerable students; and, (c) our at-risk and vulnerable students are dropping out and entering into school-to-prison pipeline. Our institutions, organizations, and communities must play their roles honorably to produce great human beings who care about others different from them (see Obiakor, 2001, 2007, 2018, 2021, 2023). For example, our educator preparation programs must thoroughly educate and prepare professionals to be culturally responsive and sensitive through pre-service and in-service processes. Rather than challenge and antagonize the diversity, equity, and inclusion (DEI) projects and programs in educator preparation programs and their colleges and universities, measurable efforts must be initiated to solidify multicultural education endeavors at all levels. DEI programs and initiatives are organizational efforts to respond to racism, inequities and disenfranchisements.

As an Igbo-Nigerian American, I understand the complexities of life because I have experienced them. However, I also understand that human-beings are capable of making it less complex and complicated by continuing to learn, grow, teach, and do more to uplift themselves and others. *No Time to Retreat* goes beyond the "White Gaze," the "Black Gaze," or any "Gaze" for that matter (Carroll, 2021; Campt, 2023; Chandler, 1998; Howell et al., 2019; Rabelo et al., 2021; Yancy, 2017). My serious view is that if we can value fellow human-beings as we value ourselves, our schools, colleges/universities, institutions, organizations, communities will be safe spaces for ALL. But, the problem is that we do not, making these spaces unsafe for ALL! Cumulatively, this book focuses on (a) highlighting the "Humanity Gaze" or human valuing; (b) appreciating the wonders of human differences; (c) interrogating the soullessness of racism, xenophobia, and other forms of bigotry; (d) affirming what human-beings can do individually and collectively to enhance multicultural education and awareness; and (e) inspiring human-beings to be inquisitive to find the intersectionality between our multicultural interactions and our global existence.

We must applaud our technological improvements all over the world—they have shown that we are more alike than different and that our differences make us unique and wonderful human-beings. Of late, in some quarters, we seem to harp on "melting into one cultural pot" even though it is naturally impossible. Sadly, in their actions, schools, colleges/universities, institutions, organizations, and communities have continued to flirt with this dangerous trend of silencing diverse and "new" voices. *No Time to Retreat* boldly urges us to make our voices heard as we appreciate and value our differences because they enrich us in multidimensional ways. In addition, it recognizes the global nature of our world by challenging educational accreditation agencies to put their monies where their mouths are. For example, while they consistently urge us to infuse global and multicultural education in all educational programs, they have rarely brought the hammer down on programs that have resisted such paradigm and power shifts. These confusing signals have continued to paralyze our true and realistic definitions of "good" schools, "good" programs, "good" institutions, "good" organizations, and "good" communities.

No Time to Retreat inspires us to respect quality without minimizing DEI-focused intentions and programs. It further presents why DEI projects and programs must be strengthened to move us forward and lay strong educational foundations for our future generalizations. As we can see today, there are blatant racist, discriminatory, and backward movements taking place in the United States. Examples include the current book banning ventures, history cleansing endeavors, fights to dismantle DEI projects, uncompromising xenophobic actions, and White supremacist puritanical directions. Unwittingly, oppositions have been mild and lacking proactive intensity. And, we can do better than that! This book vigilantly recognizes where we are and challenges us to do more and better to move us forward in solidifying functional goal-directed solutions! Clearly, this book will be a great resource to teachers and professors at all educational levels. It can serve as a major or supplementary text for undergraduate and graduate courses in regular education, special education, sociology, psychology, and international relations, to mention a few.

Finally, writing a book of this nature is challenging but cathartically rewarding—it involves reading, talking, learning, researching, deep thinking, writing, patience, and determination. I thank Dr. Sean Warner of Clark Atlanta University and Dr. Carlos McCray of Montclair State University for doing the Foreword and Afterword of this book, respectively. I also give special thanks to Emerald for believing in me. And, I immensely thank my wife and children for their powerful love and support during this venture. Again, it takes a good village to make good things happen!

Festus E. Obiakor

References

Bruni, F. (2024). *The age of grievance.* Avid Reader Press/Simon & Schuster.

Campt, T. M. (2023). *A Black gaze: Artists changing how we see.* Penguin USA.

Carroll, R. (2021). *Surviving the White gaze: A memoir*. Simon and Schuster.
Chandler, D. (1998). Notes on "the gaze". http://aber.ac.uk/media/documents/gaze//gaze.html
Howell, D., Norris, A., & Willimas, K. L. (2019). Towards Black gaze theory: How Black female teachers make Black students visible. *Urban Education Policy and Research Annals, 6*(1), 20–30.
Obiakor, F. E. (2001). *It even happens in "good" schools: Responding to cultural diversity in today's classrooms*. Corwin Press.
Obiakor, F. E. (2007). *Multicultural special education: Culturally responsive teaching*. Pearson Merrill/Prentice Hall.
Obiakor, F. E. (2008). *The eight-step approach to multicultural learning and teaching* (3rd ed.). Kendall/Hunt.
Obiakor, F. E. (2018). *Powerful multicultural essays for innovative educators and leaders: Optimizing "hearty" conversations*. Information Age.
Obiakor, F. E. (2020). *Valuing other voices: Discourses that matter in education, social justice, and multiculturalism*. Information Age.
Obiakor, F. E. (2021). *Multiculturalism still matters in education and society: Responding to changing times*. Information Age.
Obiakor, F. E. (2023). *Reducing hate through multicultural education and transformation*. Information Age.
Rabelo, V. C., Robotham, K. J., & McCluney, C. L. (2021). "Against a sharp white background": How Black women experience the white gaze at work. *Gender, Work and Organization, 28*(5), 1840–1858.
Yancy, G. (2017). *Black bodies, White gazes: The continuing significance of race* (2nd ed.). Rowman & Littlefield.

CHAPTER 1

WHY MULTICULTURALISM MATTERS IN EDUCATION AND LIFE

ABSTRACT

Multiculturalism matters, not just in education, but in life! Downplaying this fundamental exactitude is tantamount to downplaying the sacred existence of humanity. Human-beings are different and differences reflect our perceptions about our realities and changes. As critical as changes are, they can be scary. As a result, they cause confusions, collusions, and conflicts. Should we then run away from change? No! We cannot function as human-beings without change, especially if that change is productive. While multiculturalism is viewed by some skeptics as new, façade, and anti-quality, it is as old as humanity and represents a productive change that values differences in culture, language, gender, religion, ability, disability, national origin, collaborative instinct, and personal idiosyncrasy. This chapter presents why multiculturalism matters and sets the stage for the entire book.

Keywords: Multiculturalism; education and life; leadership with a heart; reducing conflict; valuing difference and change; advancing humanity

Introduction

As human beings, we have fundamental beliefs that are anchored in tradition. These beliefs can either be right or wrong depending on perceptions.

However, like most human beings, I get excited and optimistic about change even though it sometimes appears far-fetched. In some quarters, change is viewed as a reality; and in other quarters, it is viewed as a façade. Change can be a wonderful phenomenon; however, it can be scary. Thomas Friedman (2005), in his book, *The World Is Flat: A Brief History of the Twenty-First Century*, acknowledged change as life-changing and scary. As Friedman (2005) posited, while the Western World arrogantly thought that it ran the world, other people and other cultures were humbly busy working hard, educating their people, creating inventions, developing their societies, and flattening the curve of advancements. Embedded in this premise is the fact that change and productivity impinge upon sets of belief systems that are tied to human, patriotic, and national identities and priorities. In other words, change and productivity are rooted in human valuing that go hand-in-glove with culture, language, education, ability, creativity, investment, collaboration, and productivity, the powerful engines of multiculturalism. By definition, multiculturalism is a positive change-oriented tendency and willingness to learn and teach about human differences and valuing with particular attention to race, culture, language, national origin, religion, gender, ability, disability, personal idiosyncrasy, and so on (Obiakor, 2001, 2007, 2008, 2018, 2020, 2021, 2023a, 2023b, 2024a, 2024b). Additionally, multiculturalism is a life's phenomenon that is encapsulated in and intertwined with multicultural education; yet, because of its complexities, it is often misrepresented as "new," "façade," "controversial," and a tool to minimize quality. Today, in many quarters, multiculturalism is narrowly confined and simplistically attached to the rhetoric of "wokeness" and the unfairness of *diversity, equity, and inclusion* projects, investments, and programs. The facts remain that multiculturalism (a) goes beyond narrow rhetoric and simplification; (b) brings and adds much more to educational, economic, societal, and political tables; (c) demonstrates an inclusive valuing of our inter-individual and intra-individual differences; and (d) enhances, sustains, and advances our human existence (see Obiakor, 2001, 2007, 2008, 2018, 2020, 2021, 2023a, 2023b, 2024a, 2024b). Simply put, multicultural valuing is human valuing!

Our long doubts about multiculturalism might make it to look fictitious. But, it is not! I believe viewing something that is cemented in authentic reality (e.g., the air we breathe) as novelty can have some negative consequences. In earnest, multiculturalism is a reality that must be taken seriously if we are to sustain the humanity of our multicultural world. When we see and hear of all the turmoil taking place in different communities, regions, and nations of our world, we have the human urge to envelop ourselves in skepticism. The good news is that while the turmoil is going on, there are also visible signs of multidimensional advancements at all levels. For example, there are economic and technological advancements (e.g., artificial intelligence) that are being contemplated and made by gurus and leaders to move our world forward. But, our cups seem to be half-full at different levels! Rather than move forward to remediate the plights of their respective citizens, many national and world leaders in different regions of the world are perpetuating or engaging in disruptive and war-oriented threats, utterances, behaviors, and actions. Apparently, these leaders have forgotten or are forgetting history and reverting to creating disharmony, discontent, and disunity that consistently hurt our world. They seem to intentionally deemphasize collaborative, consultative, and cooperative endeavors and energies that encourage placidity. And, they go out of their ways to rule with impunity, silence voices of their fellow citizens, and create problems that are destructive to the sacred existence of their citizens and neighbors (Obiakor, 2020, 2021, 2023b). The question then is, how do we sustain the reality of multiculturalism in our multicultural world? This chapter responds to this question.

Socio-Cultural Disorientations at World-Wide Levels

World-wide, there are critical disconcerting incidents that have been exposed at micro and macro levels. These incidents have created far-reaching disruptive, disastrous, and deadly environments for harmonious human and multicultural interactions (Obiakor et al., 1997). The following sub-sections briefly expose examples of socio-cultural disorientations that call for multicultural re-orientations in the world.

In the United States of America

In the United States, we pride ourselves on being the richest and greatest democracy in the world. And, we have consistently exported our beliefs and doctrines all over the world. Our belief in FREEDOM is uncompromised; however, of late, there seems to be an overwhelming enthusiasm to value and consume grievances. This negative enthusiasm has been exploding like wild fires—everyone seems to be upset for one reason or the other even though the ramifications are far-reaching. Frank Bruni (2024), in his book, *The Age of Grievance*, decried this incessant urge to gripe at everyone, everything, and every situation. In the same context, Paul Waldman and Tom Schaller (2024), in their book, *White Rural Rage: The Threat to American Democracy* delineated the dangers of the obvious anger of rural Whites who though "poor" economically continue to blame different "others" for their plights and situations. Unfortunately, the business man turned politician, Donald Trump has taken advantage of this White anger in his racist, xenophobic, and controversial pronouncements and utterances. And, shockingly, his grievance-loaded rhetoric engineered his election as the 45th President of the country. He ran for reelection and lost to President Joseph Biden—this loss has continued to trigger increased closed-minded, hateful, right wing, and racist directions and tracks in many circles (Obiakor, 2023b). Though overwhelmed with many court cases, he won the Republican Party's nomination for Presidency which set him up to run for the position and win again.

The greatest irony in the American dilemma is the tremendous support for Donald Trump by the Christian Right wingers who do not mind his racist, xenophobic, and hateful pronouncements. For example, not long ago, Stimson (2024) puritanically urged the legal system to send more people to prison without remedial and humane solutions and accused lawyers who he called "rogue prosecutors" of not executing the laws. The obvious outcomes of these negative directions are (a) disruptive and hateful actions that have permeated our society, and (b) extreme devaluing of our country's multicultural harmony. Following are other visible problems:

- Measurable hateful and White supremacist activities.
- Magnifying presence of QAnon and other conspiracy theories.
- Shameless exaltation of right wing violent groups like the Proud Boys and Oat Keepers.
- Full-blown spread of the Replacement theory of White people.
- Irresponsible and autocratic restriction of abortion rights of women.
- Scary attack of the United States Capitol to truncate the Presidential choice of the American masses.
- Reckless uses of guns to scare, shoot, or kill other people under the respectful banner of the second amendment of the United States Constitution (i.e., the right to keep and bear arms).
- Remorseless brutalizing, shooting, jailing, and imprisoning of Blacks, especially Black males by the police and the legal system.
- Ignorant banning of books that are deemed "unfit" in libraries.
- Tremendous hate of immigrants seeking for better opportunities in the country.
- Extreme pursuit of racist, right wing, undemocratic and conservative principles and actions.

In Western European Nations

In Western Europe, socio-cultural and political centers are being threatened consistently. Consider a few examples! In the United Kingdom, conservative right-wing agitations and inclinations are operational with no regard for humanity and multiculturalism at different levels. These right-wing tentacles visibly surfaced during the 2022 election of Prime Minister Rishi Sunak, the son of a Punjabi, Indian Hindu parents born in Tanzania and Kenya who migrated to England. To respond to unsteady agitations, his obvious and underlying policies (e.g., his immigration policies) began to hover around extremism and exclusivity. Mr. Sunak's government was in so much turmoil that he and his conservative cohorts were voted out in 2024 and replaced by Prime Minister Keir Starmer and his Labour Party. Interestingly, Mr. Starmer's wife, Victoria has a Jewish heritage—this adds some multicultural texture to his regime. We can also visibly notice that White supremacist and right wing politicians and citizens are winning votes and excelling in Germany, France, and other Western European nations. While collaborative advances are made, the gates of disenfranchisements and disillusionments are opening at very fast rates. Xenophobia and other forms of protectionist behaviors are showing up everywhere (e.g., in soccer games). The good news is that life continues to go on and positive changes continue to occur!

In Eastern European Nations

In Eastern Europe, human and multicultural unrests are now on very high alert and must be handled with care to prevent another world war! For example, President Vladimir Putin of Russia has consistently demolished his political opponents (e.g., Alexei Navalny's 19 year imprisonment and death). Not long ago, Putin invaded Ukraine to take it over and prevent it from becoming a North Atlantic Treaty Organization member—this has resulted in a war that destroyed many lives and devastated economies and stabilities. Surprisingly, this invasion has caused some internal strife in Russia to the extent that on June 17, 2023, the Wagner mercenary group plotted a coup under the leadership of Yevgeny Prigozhin to show their disgruntlement about the goings-on in the war. As it appears, neighboring countries are worried, forcing them to solidify their relationship with North Atlantic Treaty Organization (e.g., Poland) and become new entrants of North Atlantic Treaty Organization (e.g., Finland and Sweden). Disruptions, disasters, and deaths are becoming daily occurrences in that part of the world.

In Asiatic Nations

In Asiatic nations, there are disruptive moves in many areas of the region (e.g., Hong Kong and Taiwan) engineered by China. As in many regions, religious minorities are victimized for practicing their faiths. While India is advancing technologically, religious minorities are victimized and the caste system is practiced quietly. In North Korea, individual freedoms are trampled upon and dictatorial dominations are publicly celebrated while opponents are killed with reckless abandon. And, in the Arab World, individual freedoms (e.g., freedom to worship and freedom to enjoy one's personal idiosyncrasies) are not very much honored. In addition, war-like disruptions are taking place in countries such as Iran, Syria, Israel, Palestine, and so on. For instance, Hamas, the dominant force in Gaza attacked Israel and killed and kidnapped many citizens and Israel retaliated also by attacking and killing many citizens in Gaza. These crises have continued to shake up and disrupt the Middle East and other parts of the world. We continue to hope that these crises could be resolved to build harmony, peace, and tranquility in that part of the world. Generally, while wealth and luxuries of civilization are manifesting themselves, visible uneasiness continues to be a reality in many parts of this region.

In African Nations

Though there are traces of growth in Africa, many of its countries are overwhelmed with perennial multicultural struggles and dilemmas. For example, national leaders in African nations seem to be very chronologically old when generally compared to leaders in the Western World. These leaders have used tribalism, religious fanaticism, and intimidations to divide their own nations, making peace and unity some farfetched ideas. In addition, there are (a) myriad tribal wars and secessionist inclinations in many African nations; (b) rampart corruptions and financial embezzlements; and (c) zero checks and balances at all systemic levels. All over Africa, there are tribal-related conflicts and wars that have been buttressed by poor leadership and myopic perspectives; and, there is the lack of suitable philosophies to guide economic, social, political, and educational directions. As a result, military coups and leaderships have resurfaced in many countries (e.g., Mali, Guinea, Burkina Faso, Gabon, and Niger), creating more room for disruptions, disasters, and deaths (Obiakor, 2023b; Obiakor et al., 1997). And, lately in Somalia and Sudan, conflicts and wars are raging on, forcing other countries to fly home their citizens and even close their embassies.

In many African nations, leadership has transitioned from military to civilian or semi-civilian rules, making it difficult to differentiate between democracy and authoritarianism. African leaders seem to have refused to learn from history; and African citizens seem to have divorced themselves from historical realities and consequences of conflicts and wars. If not, how can they allow themselves to be brutally manipulated and ruled by grossly ignorant leaders? Of late, citizens of some countries are willing to suffer, sacrifice, or even die to regain their freedoms. In countries such as Mali,

Guinea, Burkina Faso, Niger, and Gabon where the military governments took over, their citizens embraced the military for creating positive changes. What an irony? There appears to be some light at the end of the tunnel—for example, after much political hassles, Senegal just democratically elected a 44 year old man, Bassirou Diomaye Faye to be its next President.

A prime example of the perennial multicultural problems in Africa is Nigeria, my country of origin that is presumed to be the "Giant of Africa." While Nigeria is the most populated and supposedly the richest Black nation in the world and also a country that has tremendous talented people who live and excel all over the world, it continues to move backward instead of forward. For instance, it has consistently produced some of the most inept leaders in the world. For eight years, it was ruled by President Muhammadu Buhari, a Northern Fulani Muslim and former military leader who came to power by promising to destroy terrorism and socioeconomically advance the country. Throughout his rule, it became evident that he was a religious and tribal zealot who abused his power by myopically giving his critical positions and opportunities to mostly Fulani and Northern people while at the same time passionately hating the Ibos. It is now no surprise that most Nigerians, especially the Ibos view Mr. Buhari as the worst President to ever rule Nigeria. In the most recent elections supposedly won by Bola Ahmed Tinubu, a Yoruba Muslim man from the Southwest of Nigeria who also chose another Muslim man from the North as Vice President, there were bitter revelations of frauds, corruptions, divisions, intimidations, and threats against the Ibos and others. These elections led to multiple court cases that further exposed political corruptions at very high levels. Today, Nigeria's future appears to be very unclear because old wounds have been reopened and tribal divisions have exposed old hidden ills that include:

- Agitations of the Indigenous People of Biafra existing in the South Eastern parts of the country.
- General reminders about the disastrous Biafra/Nigeria war.
- Boko Haram agitations and killings that flourish in the Northern parts of the country.
- Political upheavals and socio-economic stagnations that continue to handicap the whole country.
- Uneasiness about the high poverty levels of the Nigerian citizenry.
- Blatant and gross demonstrations of combined evils of *tribalism* and *nepotism* at national leadership levels.

Looking at most of the global happenings today, it will be unrealistic to think that the world is at a solidly peaceful multicultural place. However, this does not mean that we should fold our hands and give up! What this means is that we must be proactive in educating ourselves about how we can value and respect each other in our multicultural world. We must also realize that whatever "good" or "bad" that is happening anywhere in the world affects all of us. We cannot hide from this! In other words, there must be frantic efforts to foster multicultural education and transformation at all levels (see Obiakor, 2023b). And, as a collective, we must hate "hate" by seriously instituting and stabilizing policies that will resuscitate and sustain our multicultural values (Beachum, 2023; Obiakor, 2023b).

Sustaining Our Multicultural Values to Uplift Humanity

Based on the aforementioned examples and details, it appears that the whole world has gone crazy or is going ablaze. Hate seems to be everywhere (Obiakor, 2023b); yet, everyone seems to hate hate (Beachum, 2023). I believe the world is going through some metamorphoses of growth that will in the long run shift paradigms and powers to benefit the advancement of humanity. While we have multidimensional problems, our world has people endowed with gifts and talents that can ameliorate and solve our human problems. From my perspective, our problems require multidimensional solutions that are in consonance with multicultural education and transformation (see Obiakor, 2020, 2021, 2023a, 2023b, 2024a, 2024b). The world needs educational, economic, political, and societal leaders who are transformational and multicultural at the same time. Cumulatively, these leaders must understand that:

- There is connectivity between the pillars of education and the pillars of economics, politics, and society.
- Any issue that affects the educational pillar affects the other major pillars of economics, politics, and society.
- Good leadership avoids myopic, naïve, and provincial thinking and actions.
- People's differences are the wonders of their individualities.
- When leadership functions operate with transformative and multicultural motifs, visions, and perspectives, innovative problem-solving ideas are instituted and implemented.

We must come to the realization that we owe it to ourselves to interrogate traditional assumptions that diminish multicultural valuing (Obiakor, 2024a, 2024b; Obiakor et al., 2024). Our interrogations must be (a) simple without oversimplifying the issues; (b) intense without over-killing the issues; (c) focused positively without being iconoclastic in nature; and (d) futuristic without ignoring the past or present. I argue that we ask targeted macro and micro focused questions such as: First, what "good" or "bad" multicultural lessons have we learned from history? Second, what multicultural actions are we taking right now to build harmonious relationships? And third, what multicultural plans are we making to advance humanity-related peace, progress, and prosperity? All societal institutions must ask themselves these macro and micro focused questions as they revisit their vision, mission, values, goals, and objectives. To this end, we must dedicatedly use the Comprehensive Support Model (Obiakor, 2001, 2008, 2018, 2020, 2021, 2023b) to functionally stimulate and energize personal, familial, community, school, state, national, and global inputs for the common good. With hopes and actions, these inputs will generate and enhance multicultural values, headways, and harmonies that will eventually advance and sustain our multicultural world.

It is difficult to sustain our multicultural values when we see multiculturalism as a political football instead of what it is. Our lack of understanding of the human benefits of multiculturalism has led to many current educational, socio-economic, and political problems (see Obiakor, 2024a, 2024b; Obiakor et al., 2024). These macro problems have created multidimensional micro problems. We now see unrepentant defiant leaders and people who care less about the ramifications of their actions regarding race, religion, gender, culture, language, disability, ability, skin color, personal idiosyncrasy, and disposition. These individuals erroneously see differences as deficits and think that their own differences are better that other people's differences. Additionally, these individuals see themselves as God's only supreme gifts to the world. The perceptions of these individuals are screwed up and reveal anti-human behaviors that are demeaning. More often than not, instead of being creative, dynamic, progressive, futuristic, inclusive, and global, they tend to be extremely traditional, conservative, dictatorial, exclusive, myopic, and provincial. Not surprisingly, their behaviors manifest hate, create disunity, and lead to the misperception, poor implementation, or lack of implementation of multiculturalism. The truth is that multiculturalism is sustained where freedoms reign and where people are provided with receptive, open-minded, nurturing, caring, and safe environments.

Finally, it is critical that we understand that a problem unsolved is still unsolved even when we try to sweep it under the rug. This means that we must recognize that we have a problem (or even problems) in today's multicultural world. I argue that our problems lie solely on our lack of multicultural knowledge on how to improve human and multicultural valuing. Of late, we seem to have downplayed multiculturalism at our own peril; and, the lack of its implementation has caused harm to individuals and society. Educationally, we must infuse multiculturalism into our whole curricula in all respective fields because there is a multicultural connection to all fields. With such infusion, we can solve STEM (i.e., science, technology, engineering, and mathematics), socio-economic, and political problems that confront the citizens of the world. To sustain our multicultural values, we must be about the business of interrogating our past, challenging our status quo, and prescribing solutions to advance our future. Additionally, we must make good things to happen instead of waiting for them to happen on their own. If we continue to wait for change to happen, it might not happen; and even if and when it happens, it might be too late. So, the time is now!

Conclusion

This chapter reiterates the benefits of understanding the multicultural nature of the world we live in and exposes the apparent interrelatedness of our world. Time and time again, we fail to understand how multiculturalism benefits global programs (e.g., World Health Organization). However, the COVID-19 pandemic showed the interconnectedness of the world and the dangers of not understanding this inter-connectivity. Historically, this lack of understanding has led to actions and inactions (e.g., the pogrom against the Jewish people in Germany and the Igbo people in Nigeria). While the pogrom against the Jews led to the World War, the pogrom against the Ibos led to the Nigeria/Biafra War—these disastrous wars led to the loss of millions of people. Unfortunately, it takes a global crisis to bring us back to the reality that we are a global village.

In the end, it is important that we understand what is at stake in our world today. Multicultural voices must be heard at all levels, including the publishing world. All hands must be on deck to educate and confront extreme bigoted persons and organizations bent on banning historical books because they view them to be heretical. I agree with Tony Roche (2025) of Emerald Publishing when he wrote, "Emerald is steadfast in its commitment to academic freedom, and we believe that a diversity of voices is more important than ever, if the societal challenges of our time are to be addressed through scientific progress" (p. 1). We cannot afford to give up and continue to play the traditional game of pretending to value each other. We do not; but we should! It is time we all agreed that:

- Our children and youth must be educated about the multicultural connectivity of the world.
- Our CLD and vulnerable children, their family members, and their communities must be accurately identified, assessed, labeled/categorized, placed, and educated.
- Our researchers, scholars, and educators must dedicatedly share their knowledge about the interrelatedness of our world through their works and publications.
- Our colleges and universities must respond to demographic changes by instituting and solidifying *diversity, equity, and inclusion* and other multicultural programs.

- Our world leaders must resist the temptation of being blind about our human differences on culture, language, religion, tribe, national origin, and gender, to mention a few.
- Our visibility must be qualitative and quantitative, even when we come from CLD and vulnerable backgrounds.
- Our voices must be functionally heard, even when they appear heretical.
- Our goal must be to share our different perspectives without threatening or hating the sacred existence of fellow humans.
- Our motif must be to value books like *No Time to Retreat: Why We Must Solidify Multicultural Education* with the understanding that such books and works answer our multicultural questions in thought-provoking ways that unite, educate, and motivate us.
- Our multicultural world must be saliently guarded and guided toward making functional goal-directed decisions.
- Our overall global obligation must be to consistently and positively change and advance our multicultural societies for the common good.

CHAPTER 2

WHY THE SEARCH FOR NEW MEANING MATTERS IN MULTICULTURAL EDUCATION

ABSTRACT

Human-beings are always in search of their own realities or what makes sense to them. More often than not, what makes sense to one person might not make sense to another person. In other words, what means something to someone might not mean anything to someone else. This means that there is a constant search for new meaning by different people based on their cultural and linguistic realities and personal idiosyncrasies. Such a search is never easy—it forces people to think outside-the-box, confront differences, ask questions, answer questions, and solve problems. How can we advance humanity without searching for new multicultural meanings? This chapter answers this question and discusses why this search matters.

Keywords: Searching for new meaning; asking and answering questions; solving problems; valuing differences; fostering changes; enhancing multiculturalism

Introduction

My late father, a successful business man, had the habit of asking me as a young boy some life-oriented questions such as, "*Son, do you know who you are?*" My usual response was, "*Yes. I am your son.*" He would respond, "*Yes, you are right, but, do you really know who you are? Do you really know the reasons for your existence as a human-being?*" Such conversations with my father were usually frustrating to me—they gave me some headache because they had no right or wrong answer. My father, the only child of his mother's life, went as far as the second grade in his education. However, he taught me to *THINK ANALYTICALLY*. He never objected to my responses—he always wanted me to think deeper about the meaning of my responses. I learned a lot from my interactions with my late father—they were rewarding and targeted toward life. Later in life, as a Ph.D. student, I took a course for my degree minor from my late professor, Dr. Greg Maltby who made us think beyond our imaginations. Many of my peers found this thinking professor to be very challenging. For me, I learned a lot from his educational philosophy class because of the foundations that I garnered early in life from my father. One of the required texts for Dr. Maltby's class was Viktor Frankl's (1984) book, *Man's Search for Meaning*. In this book, Frankl (1984), a Jewish man, used his prison experiences in bestial concentration camps to challenge us to make sense of our humanity and value the spirit of existentialism, meaning "to live is to suffer, to survive is to find meaning in the suffering" (p. 9). Frankl (1984) emphasized that:

> If there is a purpose in life at all, there must be a purpose in suffering and in dying. But no man [woman] can tell another what this purpose is. Each must find out for himself [herself], and must accept the responsibility that his [her] answer prescribes. If he [she] succeeds he [she] will continue to grow in spite of all indignities. (p. 9)

In life, I have learned that my father, Dr. Maltby and Frankl (1984) were right—they all understood that life has intricate variables and nuances that are worthy of comprehension, application, analysis, synthesis, and evaluation. This means that we are (and should be) active thinkers and curious participants in our lives. In addition, my father, Dr. Maltby and Frankl (1984) were right to acknowledge that critical thinking and problem-solving are intertwined with human nature, valuing, and growth. Earlier, Bronoski (1971), in his book, *The Identity of Man*, correctly opined that "man [woman] is a part of nature" (p. 2). This means that we are all obligated to make conscious efforts to think, question, and understand the reasons of our existence, similarities, differences, and collective efforts to make our multicultural world a more harmonious and less hateful place. These are the foci of this chapter.

Questions of the "Heart"

It is common knowledge that if we want answers, we must ask questions. In many arenas, asking life's important questions may be difficult and sometimes conflict oriented. However, asking questions inspires us to think deeper about life and what it entails. We make perceptual mistakes when we presume that the goal for asking questions is to find out the absolute "Black or White" or "right or wrong" answer. Our blindness on life's realities (a) disrupts our life's search for meaning, (b) discourages our meaningful conversations, (c) silences our already invisible voices, (d) stifles our scared minds, (e) forces us to search for phony truths and false prophets, and (f) creates very dangerous pathways for our humanity. In other words, asking and answering questions about our burning issues (e.g., genetic and environmental influences on our intelligence) fosters multiculturalism, buttresses our search for new answers, increases our values as human animals, and helps us to see the deeper lives of our different "others" (Gould, 1981). These are the reasons why we must continue to ask thought-provoking questions that produce unending knowledge, interactions, and solutions. This means that our unending questions yield unending truths that cyclically yield more unending questions; and these questions directly and indirectly set the stage for knowledge-seeking and problem-solving initiatives.

As humans, we need questions of the "heart" to continuously focus on ways to enhance life and humanity. It is critical that we ask and answer questions about life to advance life. These questions should include the following:

- Why are we members of the peoples of the world?
- Why are we different from other people?
- What are our similarities as human beings?
- Why do we exist?
- What is our role in personal and community survival and enhancement?
- Why should we interact and work with fellow humans?
- What can we do to advance peace and harmony and reduce war and hate?
- Why do we continue to have and encourage the disharmonies in our world today?
- Why do we have problems getting along or working for the common good?
- What defines or makes up the common good?
- Who are role models in our complex world? And, what makes them role models?

Logically, these questions might be tough and over-the-top in a world where people are deeply thinking about personal survival. Nonetheless, they are critical to our sacred existence and survival as a human race. In fact, not responding to them is like living inside a burning house and expecting not to die.

There is no doubt that the above questions challenge our human nature, intrigue our souls as human beings, and inspire or force us to engage in critical thinking that is enveloped in problem-solving. Indeed, understanding the critical nature of these life-oriented questions should motivate us to ask more pertinent questions, such as:

- Why are we still being challenged with immigration and migration problems today?
- Why do we still have hunger and poverty problems in most regions and places today?
- Why are we still struggling with the climate crises today?
- Why do we still have leaders who are not interested in building conscientious communities?
- Why are we still dealing with leaders of countries invading other countries?
- Why are we still dealing with the endemic problems of racism, gender discrimination, xenophobia, national origin, religious dogmatism, tribalism, nativism, and linguistic bigotry?
- Why do we still have the kind of pervasive ignorance of White supremacy that leads to disruptions, disasters, and deaths?

These questions might be highly loaded; however, they are real questions that deserve immediate attention to build multiculturalism in our communities, nation, and world. We cannot continue to sweep them under the rug and expect them to disappear. They will continue to disrupt our equilibrium as a society until we start dealing with them proactively, intentionally, seriously, and intensely.

Implications for Multicultural Education

We know that we cannot teach what we do not know. And, to know, we must ask and answer questions! As a result, we must continue to seek knowledge and information and teach, as needed. I believe we cannot search for new meaning without solving old problems. And, to resolve old problems, we must continue to ask questions about old traditional practices that have continued to hamper the successes of people who come from culturally and linguistically diverse (CLD) and vulnerable backgrounds.

It is clear that some of our traditional ways have failed! We truly need new ways of questioning, responding, thinking, and problem-solving to reach atypical learners (Block & Dworkin, 1976; Goleman, 1995; Obiakor, 2018, 2020, 2021, 2023b). These questions must include the following:

- Why are CLD learners still not maximizing their fullest potential in school programs?
- Why do we still misidentify, misassess, mislabel/miscategorize, misplace, and misinstruct CLD and vulnerable learners?
- Why do we still rely on IQs and continue to have the IQ controversy?
- Why are classes not still modified, differentiated, and reorganized to meet the needs of CLD and vulnerable learners?
- Why do we still not focus on emotional intelligence programs?
- Why are we still struggling with poorly prepared leaders, teachers, and related professionals?
- Why are CLD students still not graduating at the same rate as their White counterparts?
- Why are we still struggling with the recruitment, retention, tenure, and promotion of CLD professors, administrators, and staff?
- Why do we still continue to make environments unwelcoming and uncomfortable for CLD professionals and students in schools, colleges, and universities?

On the whole, we must be consistent in our search for new meaning by *asking questions, getting answers, and solving problems.* While many discriminatory problems continue to hinder educational achievements of CLD persons, we cannot all be silenced and become invisible voices whose dreams and opportunities to learn are destroyed. We must continue to ask questions and seek for answers to our lingering problems. If we do not ask probing questions, we will not know; and, if we do not know, we will not grow. Then, if we do not grow, our society, economy, politics, and education will not grow (see Obiakor, 2018, 2020, 2021, 2023a, 2023b).

Conclusion

This chapter challenges us to search for new meaning by asking critical human and life-changing questions. We cannot continue to fake it anymore by pretending that everything is beautiful while our problems continue to linger and grow. Dewey (1958, 1960) was right when he concluded that education is a continuous process of growth and an embodiment of experientialism, and experimentalism. The reality is that we cannot grow without challenging ourselves, asking questions, seeking answers, or engaging in functional goal-directed solutions; and, we short-sell ourselves when we refuse to shift our paradigms and powers. It is important that we tackle our problems to save our students, organizations, institutions, and communities. If we continue with the current multicultural games that we are playing, our education, economy, society, nation, and world will suffer. Finally, by asking and answering fundamental life-changing questions that enhance multiculturalism, we inspire and motivate ourselves and others. This means that our searches for new meaning must create (a) new ways of seeing, hearing, feeling, and talking; and (b) new avenues for us to value and love others who are different from us. In the words of Frankl (1984):

> Love is the only way to grasp another human being in the innermost core of his[her] personality. No one can become fully aware of the very essence of another human being unless he [she] loves him[her]. By his[her] love he[she] is enabled to see the essential traits and features in the beloved person; and even more, he[she] sees that which is potential in him[her], which is not yet actualized but yet ought to be actualized. Furthermore, by his[her] love, the loving person enables the beloved person to actualize these potentialities. By making him[her] aware of what he[she] can be and of what he[she] should become, he[she] makes these potentialities come true. (p. 116)

CHAPTER 3

WHY GOOD DISPOSITIONS MATTER IN MULTICULTURAL INTERACTIONS

ABSTRACT

Human-beings are different; and these differences come in different shapes and forms. In addition, these differences are connected to culture, language, national origin, religion, gender, value, ability, disability, and personal idiosyncrasy. Based on these connections, individual behavioural patterns manifest themselves and generate wonderful dispositions and not-so-wonderful or fake dispositions. While these dispositions can enhance healthy multicultural interactions; they can also create unfriendly, inimical, divisive, and hateful environments. To solve individual and group problems and build effective multicultural interactions, it is important to develop good dispositions and work hard to institute programs that enhance such dispositions. This chapter elaborates why good dispositions matter in multicultural interactions.

Keywords: Understanding dispositions; good dispositions; healthy multicultural interactions; reducing hate; developing people; building societies

Introduction

On March 20, 2024, the United Nations launched the International Day of Happiness Report to reaffirm the notion that happiness is a positive disposition that is needed to uplift humanity. In more ways than one, the

United Nations confirmed that happy people and societies are healthier, more productive, and more peaceful. This was a pleasant surprise for the body to make globally public what people, even in so-called primitive societies have known for centuries. And, it became a welcome idea for our changing world, especially since our demographic changes tend to synchronize with our socio-cultural shifts in paradigms and powers (see Obiakor, 2018, 2020, 2021, 2023a, 2023b). These shifts reveal differences in human actions, reactions, behaviors, and dispositions; and these differences force the interrogation of traditionally held beliefs and the intentional or unintentional disruption of fundamental values and strongholds.

Not surprisingly, current changes have created challenges that have not been easy to handle. In addition, they have led to soft and strong reactions to situations and circumstances in ways that have been sometimes intriguing, venomous, and at times scary. At some levels, it looks like everyone has gone crazy! While this might sound ridiculous and hyperbolic, there are clearly strange behaviors and dispositions that are taking place around the world today. Some of these behaviors and dispositions appear to be so strange and repugnant that one is left to wonder if our world is moving forward or backward. For example, in businesses, politics, churches, schools, communities, and governments, human behaviors, dispositions, and activities are getting more and more atypical and out of the ordinary. While I do not object to the atypical natures of today's behavioral and dispositional patterns, one can argue that we have forgotten that we live in a multicultural world (see Obiakor, 2018, 2020, 2021, 2023a, 2023b).

It is clear that technological advancements have been helpful in enhancing human knowledge and interactions all over the world. As we can see, whatever happens in one place, negative or positive, is seen in other places; and whether it is good or bad, it gets emulated everywhere. This means that "bad" or inappropriate and "good" or appropriate behaviors and dispositions are spread from one corner of the globe to the other. While it is difficult to police behaviors and dispositions, some technologies have been responsible for fostering hateful and anti-social behaviors and dispositions (see Obiakor, 2023b, 2024a, 2024b; Obiakor et al., 2024). Despite these revelations, we still want people to engage in behaviors and dispositions that foster human and multicultural relations; and, we still want a world where schools, communities, organizations, and institutions engage in behaviors and dispositions that value our differences, create harmonious and safe spaces, and build multicultural bridges. These are the foci of this chapter.

Understanding Dispositions

Generally, dispositions are connected to behaviors; and like behaviors, they are culturally, environmentally, situationally, and circumstantially based. They can sometimes deviate from acceptable standards, occur frequently, and have durational considerations (Obiakor & Algozzine, 1995). Usually, they are evaluated on how "good" or "bad" they are; and we judge them from our prejudicial, myopic, and narrow perspectives and lenses. Despite these intricate interpretations, there are behaviors and dispositions that actually enhance human and multicultural interactions (see Obiakor, 2018, 2020, 2021, 2023a, 2023b; Obiakor & Algozzine, 1995). What then are dispositions? According to Da Ros-Voseles and Fowler-Haughey (2007), dispositions "are frequent and voluntary habits of thinking and doing" (p. 1); and they are "environmentally sensitive—meaning they are acquired, supported, or weakened by interactive experiences in an environment…" (see Da Ros-Voseles & Fowler-Haughey, 2007, p. 1). In simple terms, a disposition can mean one's attitude or mood that may be welcoming or unwelcoming. Sadly, in our world today where the "I don't care" attitude is prevalent, an unfettered freedom of expression can lend itself to dispositions that destroy meaningful collaboration, consultation, and cooperation, the basic ingredients of human and multicultural valuing.

The question continues to be, what dispositions can foster multicultural education, behaviors, and interactions in our homes, schools, communities, nation, and world? Da Ros-Voseles and Fowler-Haughey (2007) discussed three broad types of dispositions, namely: (a) *inborn dispositions* (e.g., engaging in innate curiosity), (b) *social dispositions* (e.g., engaging in acceptability, friendliness, empathy, generosity, and cooperation), and (c) *intellectual dispositions* (e.g., engaging in problem-solving, making predictions, and surmising cause and effect relationships). As Bertram and Pascal (2002) pointed out, great dispositions include (a) *independence* (i.e., ability to self-organize or self-manage); (b) *creativity* (i.e., ability to be curious or imaginative); (c) *self-motivation* (i.e., ability to be engrossed in activities or challenges; and (d) *resilience* (e.g., ability to bounce back after set-backs or negative experiences). Though these dispositions can be mutually inclusive or mutually exclusive, they are all necessary to be successful in human and multicultural engagements, activities, and interactions.

Combating Fake Dispositions

In life, there are dispositions that are good, bad, and fake. As noted, good dispositions enhance human valuing while bad dispositions devalue humanity. However, fake dispositions tend to lack clarity (i.e., not easy to define). Also, they tend to have deceptive, confusing, self-serving, and conniving intentions. Based on these assertions, some questions come to mind. Is it possible for someone to fake his/her dispositions? Are there plastic smiles that are superficial and insincere? "Yes" is the answer to both questions! It is possible for someone to pretend to be nice to us even when he/she does not give a damn about us. Many people think it is smart to do that; however, they fail to realize that we know when people are real or fake, sincere or insincere, and non-deceptive or deceptive. In many classrooms, work places, and communities that are not well-schooled about diversity and equity issues, fake dispositions run wild. Funny enough, those who engage in them do not know that others know that they are insincere and that fake dispositions create false prophecy and fraudulent multiculturalism that are antithetical to developing programs, building bridges, and advancing communities (Obiakor, 2001, 2007, 2018, 2020, 2021, 2023b).

Fake dispositions lead to "good" or "bad" interpretations. As indicated, they are tricky and cannot be trusted just as the individuals who engage in them. People seem to think that there is political wisdom in engaging in fake dispositions; however, what is forgotten is that there is also political wisdom in pretending to accept fake dispositions. People are frequently hurt by those who engage in fake dispositions, especially if they trusted them. To a large measure, fake dispositions are deceptive means to masquerade people's realities, real feelings, and real intentions. Simply, they fool people! However, I agree with Abraham Lincoln who during his September 2, 1858 debate with Stephen A. Douglas in Clinton, Illinois famously noted that "*you can fool all the people some of the time and some of the people all the time, but you cannot fool all the people all the time.*" These two men intensely battled over the pros and cons of slavery; and the winning results of these debates catapulted Lincoln to win the Presidency of the United States.

Fake dispositions are used by all kinds of people to achieve their selfish ends. In other words, they go beyond all kinds of boundaries. Based on my personal experiences, people who are honest, sensitive, and open-minded rarely engage in fake behaviors and dispositions. And, those who are racist, xenophobic, supremacist, hateful, and soulless pretend a lot—these individuals (a) try their very best to hide their uncaring and hateful behaviors and dispositions, (b) rationalize a lot, and (c) come up with one reason or another for hating another human being. For example, in many schools, colleges/universities, institutions, organizations, and communities, the use of fake dispositions to victimize others is rampant and sometimes condoned as an administrative style. Consider the following cases:

The Case of Ms. PH

Ms. PH was a Black female who worked as an assistant to a White female Director hired in a community college that was attached to a Research 1 University in the Southwestern part of the United States. Like most community colleges, it created pathways for people interested in (a) continuing their education to four year colleges, (b) getting extra enrichment training for job promotions, and (c) getting vocational skills' certificates that prepared them for employment (e.g., secretary, computer specialist, plumber, mason, car mechanic, and electrician). Ms. PH was a true professional who understood her job, was dedicated to excellent work, and took it seriously. This Director had the frequent habit of telling people how she loved Latino and Black cultures. It was a game that she consistently played. She talked about how she loved Black musicians like Lionel Richie and Bob Marley. By the same token, she had the habit of firing Latinos and Blacks who worked under her and hiring White workers at very frequent rates. Before long, she seriously tried to fire Ms. PH; and Ms. PH reported her to her Chief Executive Officer. It happened that the institution had been documenting her negative and prejudicial activities. This Director was reprimanded and warned to desist from engaging in behaviors and dispositions that are antithetical to her job responsibilities. However, she could not change and she was fired!

The Case of Mrs. R

Mrs. R worked as a middle level program coordinator in a Research 1 University. She was an African immigrant to the United States and married to a popular lawyer in the city. She pretended to be a social butterfly that wanted to be loved by everyone. But, she had some very dangerous habits of (a) being arrogant and pompous, (b) having respect for White co-workers and no respect for Blacks of any type, (c) thinking that she was smarter than everyone, (d) being very jealous of her co-workers, especially those that she supervised, and (e) treating some preferred workers better than others. In fact, she was always saying that she never knew what one of her workers particularly did on the job, even though she was one of the best employees in that department. She played her staff against each other, rewarded some workers, and disrespected family members of her colleagues. Simply, she was extremely power conscious. Even though she pretended to be a nice person who was a social butterfly, climate and discriminatory cases were consistently filed against her in the university's equity department. Additionally, though she had very negative, divisive, and unproductive dispositions, she was consistently protected and given promotional and leadership opportunities by the university for reasons that are unknown. Mrs. R's situation was so unbearable that most of the department's staff began to quit; and, the department continued to struggle with her leadership style.

Case of Ms. A

Ms. A was an African American female Director of combined remedial programs at a major Research 1 University who was hired because the acting Director was not viewed as a kind and likeable individual and leader. In addition, the acting Director was too straight forward and showed no emotional attachment to anyone. Ms. A pretended to show some emotional connections which presented her as caring leader. Unfortunately, her emotions were phony and detached. She had the habit of crying with an employee; yet, she did not hesitate to stab him/her in the back. It was difficult to read Ms. A at first; but, as situations continued in the work place, her heartlessness, wickedness, soullessness, and carelessness began to unveil themselves. She began to be viewed as a diabolic human being—she could not build harmony and broad relationship as a leader. Her behavioral dispositions began to disrupt the work place to the extent that the university authorities began to pay attention. When she found out that a drastic action would be taken against her, she decided to retire abruptly.

In the above details, we have cases of people who thrived with fake and deceptive dispositions. These people pretended to care; but, they did not care. Though they pretended to be multicultural, they were not! As evident, people with fake dispositions typically think that they are more intelligent and brighter than others. But, they are not! The fact remains that they are more dangerous than they know since they are not interested in building conscientious communities. These deceptive individuals are usually unkind, unclear, insidious, wicked, patronizing, and hateful. Looking at the Case of Ms. PH, we see a dedicated professional who was focused on doing her job; and, we also see her Director who pretended to be culturally sensitive, but was not! In fact, this Director was racist toward her colleagues and those that she supervised. In the Case of Mrs. R, we see a lady who forgot that she was an immigrant. Even though she pretended to be social, she was hateful and closed-minded. In the Case of Ms. A, we see a lady who was an expert in faking her dispositions. How can someone cry with an employee and at the same hate him/her? That is pretty heartless! These critical details call for necessity strategies to enhance positive dispositions at all levels, including schools, colleges/universities, workplaces, and communities.

Enhancing Positive Dispositions

We know that positive dispositions can enhance multicultural interactions; and, we also know that positive dispositional interactions can be taught, learned, and practiced. As a society, we downplay and ignore the roles of good dispositions in advancing education and society. Clearly, our positive dispositions are tied to our caring, kind, and sensitive emotions. Good dispositions are not based on rhetoric—they are based on action-oriented values. Consider the following example:

The Case of Dr. E

My eye doctor, Dr. E. was a White male who was always nice and respectful to me, a Black man with foreign accent. I frequently had good fearless conversations with him and always appreciated his positive dispositions. Not long ago, I had my cataract surgery. After my surgery, I was pleasantly surprised to receive some beautiful flowers from him and his colleagues. He did not have to do that; but, he did! I was so pleased that my pains suddenly disappeared and my fears about the after-effects of the surgery diminished because of the doctor's positive dispositions.

Though it could have been easy to moralize or rationalize Dr. E.'s behaviors and dispositions above, as a patient, I was convinced that I was in the good hands of a good doctor. The ways that he treated me brought so much peace to me and rejuvenated my feelings and spirits. Linda Greyman (2025), the founder of *The Minds Journal*, was right in one of her popular inscriptions: "*Health does not always come from medicine. Most of the time it comes from peace of mind, peace of the heart, peace of the soul. It comes from laughter and love.*" In our narrow confines, Dr. E.'s behaviors could be misconstrued and misinterpreted. However, beyond our narrow confines, we can agree that he demonstrated that he (a) was a "good," kind, caring, and sensitive human-being; (b) valued his fellow human-being despite their differences in culture, language, national origin, and personal idiosyncrasy; and (c) understood that dispositions are valuable pillars for successful professional and multicultural engagements and interactions. A logical extension is that dispositions can (a) make or break good or bad perceptions of people, and (b) enhance or diminish multicultural education and interactions at all forums and levels. This means that people can be hired, fired, promoted, or demoted based on their dispositions.

It should be no surprise that all professions require some form of dispositions to be successful in them. Bertram and Pascal (2002) and Katz and Raths (1985, 1986) agreed that dispositions are necessary to prepare great human beings, including students and teachers. Ironically, most Educator Preparation Programs focus more on knowledge and skills than on dispositions of potential educators. This retrogressive habit goes hand-in-glove with traditional educational systems that focus on traditional models of viewing constructs such as "intelligence," "goodness," and "giftedness." We must understand that making an "A" grade does not mean that a person is intelligent, good, and gifted. Surprisingly, we continue to have educators, professors, administrators, leaders, and people around the world that though brilliant are "soulless" or "heartless." Bertram and Pascal (2002) confirmed that "when program expectations focus primarily on knowledge and skill, important dispositions are often ignored" (p. 3). In other words, trying to undermine the importance of positive dispositions diminishes the focus on continuous education, lifelong learning, and human interactions (Katz & Raths, 1985, 1986).

In our changing world, it is critical to target dispositions that enhance human learning such as multicultural education and interactions. The craziness that we see in the world today via technology (e.g., tiktok) can be positively or negatively eye-popping; and, assumptions, conspiracy theories, and repugnant behaviors that hamper multicultural education and interactions seem to be running wild. While we now see so much, learn so much, doubt so much, agree so much, and disagree so much based on our curiosity, we cannot deny that we are also frequently misled, misinformed, and miseducated about certain realities. We can now legitimately ask, Where is the accountability? Who are our news' informants? Who are our role models? What kinds of dispositions do these role models exhibit? These are critical questions that deserve some answers, especially at all educational levels.

It is crystal clear that we now see demographic shifts in paradigms and powers—attention is now focused on improving diversity, equity, and inclusion (DEI) programs in schools, businesses, organizations, and institutions. However, we are witnessing disruptive and disastrous behaviors and dispositions of many leaders who should be making the world a good space to live in. We now see wars and deaths in most regions of the world (e.g., Russia/Ukraine and Middle East). Furthermore, there are visible and menacing manifestations of racism, xenophobia, tribalism, religious dogmatism, nativism, and hate (see Obiakor, 2023b). All of these create avenues for more people to be unhappily disenfranchised, disadvantaged, disillusioned, and demeaned. To remedy these situations, we need to prepare educators and leaders who can develop innovative programs to educate people about engaging in positive dispositions that foster multicultural education and interactions (see Obiakor, 2018, 2020, 2021, 2023a, 2023b). This means that educational leaders must measurably focus on infusing the following targeted dispositions into their programs:

- *Curiosity*—willingness to learn new knowledge.
- *Acceptability*—accepting different "others" and situations.
- *Empathy*—ability to be kind and go into the mind's eyes of others.
- *Generosity*—willingness to selflessly give.
- *Cooperation*—ability to work with others.
- *Problem solving*—willingness to resolve conflict and deal with strange situations.
- *Independence*—ability to feel free, think, and do.
- *Creativity*—willingness to create and develop.
- *Self-motivation*—ability to be self-responsible and inspired.
- *Resiliency*—willingness to be determined despite the odds.

On the whole, we must understand that dispositions are useful in fostering human and multicultural education, values, and interactions. Rather than the craziness that is prevalent in today's world, educators and other related professionals must aim at producing human beings who happily care about "others" in spite of who they are, where they come from, what they believe in, and other differences that they bring to the table (see Obiakor, 2018, 2020, 2021, 2023a, 2023b, 2024a, 2024b; Obiakor et al., 2024). Knowledge and skills are important; but, they are not enough. Good dispositions are needed to be successful in life; and we need educators and professionals with caring, kind, and happy souls and hearts. While we cannot always police behaviors and dispositions, we must encourage behaviors and dispositions that make our schools, communities, nation, and world better environments.

Since dispositions frequently manifest themselves as attitudes and behaviors, it is critically important to understand their impacts on life. Charles Swindoll (2012), in his poem, "Attitude" rightly delineated the roles of attitudes on personal lives below:

Attitude

The longer I live, the more I realize the impact of attitudes on life. Attitude, to me, is more important than facts. It is more important than the past, than education, than money, than circumstances, than failures, than successes, than what other people think, say or do. It is more important than appearance, giftedness or skill. It will make or break a company...a church...a home. The remarkable thing is we have a choice everyday regarding the attitude we embrace for that day. We cannot change out past...we cannot change the fact that people will act in a certain way. We cannot change the inevitable. The only thing we can do is play the one string we have, and that is our attitude...I am convinced that life is 10% what happens to me and 90% how I react to it. And so it is with you...we are in charge of our Attitudes.

Conclusion

As humans, we consistently wonder why some people succeed more than others; and, we also wonder why some behaviors and dispositions are more accepted, respected, and valued than others. While many might couch these interpretations as perceptions, behaviors and dispositions have consequences that can make or break people. The fact remains that there are behaviors and dispositions that matter in life because they help us to survive our trials and tribulations. And, as we move forward to solve educational, societal, and human problems, we must prepare our citizens, students, faculty, and leaders to learn and develop dispositions that enhance human and multicultural relations and interactions. Finally, the more we produce kind, caring, and happy people who can value and interact with others, the better we can measurably advance our schools, colleges/universities, institutions, organizations, communities, and nation.

CHAPTER 4

WHY SPIRITUALITY MATTERS IN MULTICULTURAL EDUCATION

ABSTRACT

From time immemorial, spirituality has been a part of life. In many quarters, spirituality has been equated with religiosity; and, most faiths connect themselves to both religiosity and spirituality. Though some religions have been exemplary in their words and deeds, some have not been exemplarily good in their historical and current actions. In reality, there are spiritual behaviors that people expect from traditional and non-traditional religions. Without favoring one religion over another, people expect religious people to be caring, kind, and humane. But, this has not always been the case. It is no surprise that problems of prejudice, misidentification, misassessment, mislabeling, racism, and hate continue to befall families, schools, and communities. To minimize problems that hamper multiculturalism, especially in school programs, it is imperative that educators and related professionals produce spiritual and caring people who can work with different "others." This chapter reiterates why spirituality matters in multicultural education and other related life activities.

Keywords: Spirituality; Christian faith and other faiths; general and special education; multicultural education; caring and kind behaviors; harmonious environments

Introduction

Not long ago, on November 20, 2023, Neo-Nazi members and White supremacists arrogantly and intimidatingly marched in downtown Madison, the capital of the State of Wisconsin, and a town that houses one of the top Research 1 Universities in the nation and world. During the march, these members invoked the name of God and Christian fundamentalist attributes. Following are probing questions that came to mind:

- What God are these people invoking? Is he the same God that I worship as a Christian?
- Is there another God that they are talking about?
- Do these people have children? What are they teaching their children?
- Do they have jobs? If they have jobs, are they teachers, lawyers, police men/women, fire fighters, engineers, journalists, civil servants, medical doctors, nurses, and so on?
- How do they relate to their co-workers who are atypical and different?
- If they are supervisors, do they hire people from culturally and linguistically diverse (CLD) backgrounds? Do they fairly recruit, evaluate, retain and promote these people?
- Where do these people live? Do they live in remote areas or in the city around CLD people?
- Do they have friends who are of different races, cultures, languages, national origins, values, and religions? How do they interact with them?
- What informs how these Neo-Nazi members live their lives or do what they do?
- What inspires someone to behave in ungodly ways and yet invoke God's name?

As I indicated, the march was extremely scary; and, it was clear that it was emotionally devastating to students, faculty, staff, administrators, and leaders of the university and community, especially those CLD people who come from different parts of the State, nation, and world. Sadly, the march reminded me of the wicked lynching of fellow human-beings and the disruptive imagery of Ku Klux Klan (KKK) members burning crosses in front of people's homes. KKK is an American Protestant-led Christian, extremist, white supremacist, far-right hate group. This KKK march made me wonder about the many evils done in the name of God and the many goods done in the name of God. All these thoughts motivated more to make a positive difference in the lives of others. On that day of the march, many of my White mentors and mentees from all over the nation called to see how my family and I were doing. I expressed my gratitude to them and promised them that I will continue to do "good" in our complex world. As a Christian who was reacting to this trauma, I began to read the Bible more to understand its deeper contextual values. During this reading period, I fell in love with many portions of the Bible. For example, I learned a lot from the Sermon on the Mount because of its emphases on humility, righteous living, integrity, loving our enemies, forgiving others, and caring about poor and disenfranchised people (Thomas Nelson, Inc., 1994); all of these are critical multicultural principles and values that are worthy of emulation and practice. The more and deeper I read, the more I learned and got convinced that the Bible and other religious books (e.g., Koran, Torah, Book of Mormon, Vedas, and Quaker Faith and Practice) could be used as excellent supplementary texts for multicultural education courses. This logically means that spirituality and education can go together; and, appreciating this connection makes it imperative to understand the contextual values of spiritual discourses and stories that elevate the caring and love of other human beings. This chapter drives this point home.

Spirituality and Education: Making the Connections

Following the spiritual directions of "treating others as you will like to be treated" and "loving thy neighbor as you love thyself" (Thomas Nelson, Inc., 1994), I believe spirituality is a major educational pillar of human valuing. For example, using the Bible as a unique educational tool, I am reminded of the Beatitudes (see Thomas Nelson, Inc., 1994, Matthew 5, 3–10) that state:

Blessed are the poor in spirit,
for theirs is the kingdom of heaven.
Blessed are those who mourn,
for they shall be comforted.
Blessed are the meek,
for they shall inherit the earth.
Blessed are those who hunger and thirst for righteousness,
for they shall be filled.
Blessed are the merciful,
for they shall obtain mercy.
Blessed are the peacemakers,
for they shall be called sons [daughters] of God.
Blessed are the pure in heart,
for they shall see God.
Blessed are those who are persecuted for righteousness' sake,
for theirs is the kingdom of heaven.

Clearly, we can learn a lot from the Beatitudes above, irrespective of our religious affiliation or denomination. They are the main theses of the biblical Sermon on the Mount that makes up the spiritual engine of the Bible. In fact, they go beyond the Bible and appear in different ways in other religious texts (e.g., Koran, Torah, and Book of Mormon). Additionally, the Beatitudes have stood the test of time because of their human inspiration to do well and human motivation to engage in higher levels of critical thinking as higher primates. In more specific terms, the Beatitudes imply that we should cumulatively extend our soulfulness, happiness and kindness to others, especially to those who are disenfranchised, disadvantaged, disillusioned, and demeaned. When people are in at risk, vulnerable, or desperate situations, simply psychoanalyzing or labeling them is not an enough solution—in fact, it adds to the problem! Sadly, this actually is what happens to many people from CLD and vulnerable backgrounds in school programs (Freire, 1996; Palmer, 1998). Though such negative experiences can be sometimes unintentional, they have devastating effects on fellow human beings. This means that educators and related professionals must have good moral compass to do the needful in their classrooms, schools, and communities. A logical extension is that it is immoral and unprofessional for educational professionals to spend time talking bad about students and their families in *faculty lounges*.

Building spiritual strengths in educators and related professionals can be beneficial to persons from CLD and vulnerable backgrounds (Obiakor, 2018, 2020, 2021, 2023b, 2024a, 2024b; Obiakor et al., 2024). Elsewhere, I addressed how my faith and culture have affected my teaching, scholarship, service, and leadership (see Obiakor, 2018). I noted that

> ...as a teacher, scholar, and leader, I have discovered that my ability to do what I do is a spiritual blessing from God, and as a result, it behooves me as a teacher-scholar and servant leader to use my professional acumen and moral compass to uplift humanity and foster human valuing. (Obiakor, 2018, p. 88)

In addition, I noted that:

> .....I fully embrace the Parable of the Good Samaritan and the Parable of the Sower. These parables inspire me to consistently be good to others, even those different from me. In addition, they motivate me to believe in "quality with a heart" in my teaching, advising, and mentoring duties. Simply put, they foster my positive belief in integrity, decency, fairness, caring, and human valuing. As a servant leader and teacher educator, I am inspired to engage in consequential or meaningful research that makes a difference in my teaching, service, and profession. (Obiakor, 2018, p. 89)

Based on the above details, it is easy to argue that all school programs must have the c-factor (i.e., caring factor)—caring has some spiritual connectivity. Obviously, there is a lack of caring or morality when we intentionally misidentify, misassess, mislabel/miscategorize, misplace, and misinstruct students (Obiakor, 2001, 2007, 2008, 2018, 2020, 2021, 2023b, 2024a, 2024b). Though caring is a fluffy idea that is difficult to measure, it does not lower quality—it enhances it and actually motivates people to work hard to achieve quality performance. Following are brief synopses of responsibilities that must be targeted in school programs:

Pre-kindergarten Program Level

At the pre-kindergarten level, educators and related professionals should design and teach head start classes thoroughly in order to prepare students for kindergarten. At this level, focusing on test scores alone is disastrous; and labeling or categorizing pre-kindergarteners is even more dangerous (Obiakor, 2001, 2007, 2024a, 2024b; Obiakor et al., 2024a). It is critical to get them interested in school by making it a safe space for multidimensional discussions about caring, love, and games. It is important for educators and related professionals to work collaboratively and consultatively with parents and introduce both parents and students to cultural and linguistic acceptance, appreciation, and valuing (Obiakor, 2001, 2007, 2008, 2018, 2020, 2021, 2023b, 2024a, 2024b).

Kindergarten Level

At the kindergarten level, students should be taught by well-trained and well-prepared teachers and professionals. All learning environments must be culturally sensitive and responsive; and team work approach must be fostered at all critical moments. At this level, learning should not be focused on testing alone; and, students' capabilities should be nurtured with care, love, and kindness. Robert Fulghum (1990) thoroughly explicated these values in his book, *All I Really Need to Know I Learned in Kindergarten: Uncommon Thoughts on Common Things* and made the case for starting very early to teach foundational humane lessons that can enhance human respect and valuing. This means that collaborative voices of students, teachers, and family/parents should be heard and that all instructions must highlight the real "goodness" of people. To a large measure, kindergarten should be a no-label environment that allows students to value others as they prepare to maximize their human potential (Obiakor, 2001, 2007; Obiakor et al., 2024).

Elementary School Level (Grades 1–6)

At the elementary school level, it is imperative to focus on the excitement about education. Instructions should be differentiated, modified, adapted, and culturally responsive to meet the needs of students. Again, at these grade levels, students should be challenged with care, kindness, and civility. And, there must be low tolerance for insensitivity, racism, xenophobia, and inflexibility by educators and related professionals (Obiakor, 2001, 2007, 2008, 2018, 2023b, 2024a, 2024b). Classes must be inclusive unless the needs are so "specially" required to facilitate learning and growth.

Middle School Level (Grades 7–8)

At the middle school level, students are now teenagers who are prone to teenage behavioral patterns. They resist rules and regulations and frequently engage in anti-social behaviors. And, teachers and other related professionals must be careful in misidentifying, misassessing, mislabeling/miscategorizing, misplacing, and misinstructing them, especially when they come from CLD and vulnerable backgrounds (Obiakor, 2001, 2007, 2018, 2020, 2023b, 2024b). If care is not taken, these students drop-out of school, consume and deal on drugs, and run into problems with law enforcement entities. However, with good and spiritual counseling and programming, these students can change and readjust. In addition, suspending and expelling them from school might set the stage for the school-to-prison pipeline.

High School Level (Grades 9–12)

At the high school level, students are preparing themselves for college and university. This new focus can create some stressors on students and teachers. As a result, strange inappropriate behaviors will resurface; and, at times, dropping out becomes an option. For students with special needs, instructions must be modified and adapted to maximize their fullest potential. Efforts must be made to be caring, kind, and sensitive to them (Freire, 1996; Obiakor, 2001, 2007, 2008, 2018, 2020, 2023b, 2024b; Palmer, 1998). To boost DEI programming, frantic efforts must be made to infuse cultural responsiveness in student, faculty, and staff treatments. And, suspension, expulsion, and school-to-prison pipeline must be resisted as much as possible. Parents must be involved and empowered to participate and collaborate with high school personnel (e.g., counselors). And, learning environments must be inviting, welcoming, and receptive without prejudicial inclinations.

College/University Level

At the college/university level, proactive efforts must be made to recruit, retain, and graduate students. DEI programs must be instituted to make sure that traditional barriers to college achievements are reduced and eliminated. To a large extent, innovative programs must be designed to make the campus more culturally responsive. Additionally, the environment must be caring and everyone must be given the opportunity to be a visible participant whose voice cannot be prejudicially silenced. Caring must be the center-piece of education and instructional programming (Freire, 1996; Obiakor, 2001, 2007, 2008, 2018, 2020, 2021, 2023b, 2024, 2024b; Palmer, 1998). The recruitment, retention, tenure, and promotion of faculty, staff, administrators, and leaders from CLD backgrounds must be efficiently, fairly, and non-discriminatorily pursued at all institutional levels (Obiakor, 2023b, 2024b). And, multicultural relationships must be built at university and community levels to boost positive visibility that is centered on "quality with a heart."

Conclusion

This chapter has discussed the relationship between spirituality, education, and human valuing. It further uses biblical allusions to address how our spirituality can help us to deal with racism, bigotry, discrimination, xenophobia, and other negative actions. It is important that we present human valuing for what it really means without judging and labeling others. Additionally, we must resist the dishonest and disingenuous nature of current discourse in education today (e.g., criticizing the DEI project and the banning of books). What is more burdensome is hearing some so-called religious people misuse or misinterpret biblical allusions to do "bad" instead of "good" things. It is disconcerting to see the political divide in the United States and our world today or when people divorce themselves from their human and spiritual realities. Furthermore, it is especially disheartening and confusing when I hear Christians and other religious people indicate that "we are all created equal" and still view different "others" as unfit, inferior, and undeserving. Sadly, in many instances, the same Christians and religious people engage in ruthless hateful behaviors and dispositions while still believing that (a) good deeds prepare us for heaven; (b) bad deeds prepare us for hell; and (c) medium range deeds prepare us for purgatory (i.e., a place of purification before going to heaven). As a teacher, scholar, professional, and leader, I believe we must infuse some spiritual contexts in students' education and growth from pre-kindergarten to university levels. To achieve our goals, we must also (a) be "hearty" in whatever we do, (b) do things that will inspire posterity to remember us, and (c) imagine what will happen to our reputation when we live this earth. This means that we are obligated to shift our paradigms and powers and systemically recalibrate our actions to be caring, kind, and sensitive as we meet the needs of *ALL* people around us.

CHAPTER 5

WHY DIVERSITY, EQUITY, AND INCLUSION PROJECTS AND INITIATIVES MATTER IN EDUCATION

ABSTRACT

Diversity, equity, and inclusion (DEI) are constructs that are entrenched in human existence. They are the functional tools that booster schools, families, communities, organizations, and institutions. And, they are central to common purpose, unity-of-purpose, and purposeful projects, initiatives, and goals. To a large measure, DEI initiatives acknowledge the (a) uniqueness in differences, perspectives, and abilities of peoples; (b) togetherness in building and rebuilding ideas and strengths of peoples; and (c) wisdom in proactively practicing the old African adage, "It takes a village to raise a child." With all the positive benefits of DEI initiatives, there are skeptics who believe it is anti-White and anti-quality. While no initiative is a panacea to solving our student, school, family, community, institutional, and organizational problems, DEI projects and initiatives have produced far-reaching and valued-added benefits to all stakeholders. This chapter discusses why these projects and initiatives matter at all educational, organizational, and institutional levels.

Keywords: DEI projects and initiatives; general and special education; valuing differences and strengths; developing multicultural programs; building inclusive organizations and institutions; fostering growth

Introduction

This chapter begins with the intriguing question, Who in the right mind will be against *DIVERSITY, EQUITY,* and *INCLUSION* (*DEI*) in a multicultural nation? My presumption is that no one in the right mind will publicly disagree with these three constructs. Sadly, as reasonable as these constructs might be, there are many people who are shamelessly against them even though they truly define human caring, goodness, soulfulness, sensitivity, and valuing. DEI projects and initiatives should be natural to many of us in a multicultural nation like the United States!

As an Igbo-Nigerian immigrant to the United States, I see DEI as a part of my life. I have been married for 42 years plus to an American who also emigrated from Jamaica, a British colonized nation. We have four American children who were raised to master the Ibo-Nigerian, Jamaican, and American cultures. My wife and I met as students at the Black Program of New Mexico State University, Las Cruces. Looking back, the Black Program was an authentic DEI program and safe space where Black students got together to study, do school assignments, exhale amicably, and interact mutually with each other. Many lifelong alumni memberships, friendships, relationships, and marriages began in such programs, spaces, and centers such as the Black Program. One can measurably argue that such programs have continued to yield value-added benefits to predominantly White college and university campuses. Coming back to my family, we operationally function from the DEI perspectives—we are multidimensional people who have different personal idiosyncrasies and who also enjoy multidimensional ways of living, thinking, learning, teaching, and doing. So, like many other families, DEI living and thinking are a part of our realities as human beings! Our family belief system is centered on the fact that everything about life is connected to DEI; and rightly so!

Based on DEI perspectives, we now see businesses, politics, educational institutions, organizations, economies, communities, and societies that are connecting themselves to DEI philosophies. DEI projects have powerful sensibilities that have great potential to advance our national character (Dukach, 2022; Washington, 2022a, 2022b; Werklabs, 2022). To a large measure, the operational engine of the DEI is cemented in humanity; and humanity, as we know it, cannot function without the collaborative efforts of different components or entities. Not only are these connections mutually inclusive, they are also mutually exclusive; and ignoring any component or entity might result in overall systemic devastation and ruins. Put another way, we cannot function and produce at intense levels as a multicultural society when we refuse to advance human collaboration, consultation, and cooperation (Obiakor, 2018, 2020, 2021, 2023a, 2023b). When "all hands are on deck," productivity rises and everyone wins! Such teamwork maximizes the growth potential of families, businesses, schools, organizations, institutions, and communities. Arguably, DEI projects and initiatives add incentives in cost effective manners and create "win, win" situations at all levels. To a large extent, these benefits challenge the notion that we should divorce DEI projects and initiatives from our daily functions as human beings. This chapter expands this notion.

Contextual Frameworks of DEI Projects and Initiatives

As indicated, DEI projects and initiatives encompass and engender *DEI*; non-complex constructs that are easy to explain or define. For purposes of clarity, *diversity* entails respecting differences in race, culture, skin color, gender, ethnicity, language, and so on; *equity* entails fairness, impartiality, equal rights, justice, and so on; and, *inclusion* entails providing equal access, state or action of including, and so on (Dunn, 2020; Urwin, 2024). Looking at these explanations, one can surmise that they are all intertwined with non-discriminatory, interdisciplinary, multidisciplinary, and multidimensional actions that are tied to human rights, human valuing, human involvement, and human inclusion in taking advantage of opportunities. In connecting the dots, THE HUMAN BEING is directly and clearly central to DEI projects and initiatives—these are especially befitting for a majority Christian nation like the United States.

It is important to note that all mainstream ideas have contextual frameworks; and, these frameworks usually have different interpretations and presentations. For example, incidents usually initiate conflicts, thereby forcing people to attach their emotions to them. Based on emotions, advocacies might spring up, thereby forcing people, leaders, and politicians to shift paradigms and powers. When movements begin to happen, litigations take place, thereby forcing responses and legislations to be initiated. It is no secret that people from culturally and linguistically diverse (CLD) and vulnerable backgrounds, especially Blacks have consistently complained for years about racism in the workplace and police brutally and killings in their respective communities; but, responses have been "half-baked" or even "unbaked." When George Floyd was killed by the police on March 25, 2020, there was a world-wide outrage. There were banners and marches expressing frustration over and condemnation of police brutality or killing. In fact, many of the banners had inscriptions such as "Never Again." It was fascinating to see that private and public responses were unified all over the world to the extent that measurable actions had to be taken. For example, sports leagues and teams all over the world represented themselves well on this outrageous act. All societal sectors (e.g., the business sector) began to positively respond to make sure that measurable changes occurred everywhere. Private and public sectors were in unison in their positive responses. A few years later, we are now going back to square-one! We are seeing some dimming of the lights on issues pertaining to DEI projects and initiatives. Apparently, many educational, business, financial, political, and social sectors are reducing and even eliminating their efforts. Sadly, the Affirmative Action dilemmas of yester years have befallen today's DEI projects and initiatives, making it difficult to institute or grow to maturity the very few positive gains that have been made.

DEI projects and initiatives have pushed the envelope in advancing antiracist policies in all facets of the United States. Departments have been created and people have been hired to manage these departments to develop consistent policies that would enhance DEI. While it appears that positive things and events are taking place, this forward-looking trend has turned backwards. In many quarters today, there are retrenchments; and, institutions, organizations, communities, States, and nation are not acknowledging the value-added benefits of DEI projects and initiatives. Although scholars and educators (e.g., Dukach, 2022; Dunn, 2020; Urwin, 2024; Washington, 2022a, 2022b; Werklabs, 2022) have made such acknowledgments, some people and organizations have continued to be skeptical about the advantages of advancing DEI projects and initiatives at all levels. Dukach (2022) indicated that:

> No matter where in the world or the power structure we find ourselves, we all have a part to play in identifying and remedying inequity. While it's easy to lose hope or descend into anger and cynicism, we're all better served by working together to listen, understand, and improve ourselves and our workplaces. And there's so much to be done—so let's stop rolling our eyes and get to it. (p. 5)

Despite the realities of DEI projects and initiatives, they have become loaded with extreme controversies and oppositions in the American society. One of those oppositions came from Heather MacDonald (2024) who in her fiery article titled, "Disparate Impact Thinking Is Destroying Our Civilization" argued that "we need to face up to the truth: the reason for racial underrepresentation across a range of meritocratic fields is the academic skills gap. The reason for racial underrepresentation in the criminal justice system is the crime gap" (pp. 4–5). In addition, MacDonald (2024) used the general 13% of the Black population in the United States to elucidate her venomous White supremacist assertions. In the words of MacDonald (2024):

> We can argue about why these disparities exist and how to close them—something that policy makers have been trying to do for decades. But in light of these skills gaps, it is irrational to expect 13 percent black representation on a medical school faculty or among a law firm's partners under meritocratic standards. At present you can have proportional diversity or you can have meritocracy. You cannot have both. (p. 5)

MacDonald's (2024) concluded her article by noting that "lowering standards helps no one since high expectations are the key to achievement. In defense of excellence we must speak the truth, never apologize, and never back down" (p. 7). Clearly, this piece glaringly and vehemently (a) opened doors for new moral and ethical questions that the White majority and our general society should answer; (b) argued that equity and quality cannot go hand-in-glove in a multicultural society; and (c) exposed the shamelessness of the White supremacist doctrine that is pervasive in exclusive and even mainstream quarters. It is unfortunate that MacDonald (2024) stooped so low to believe in fake and narrow meritocratic standards that devalue fellow human beings. Sadly, such negative noises about DEI are now so deafening, scary, and disruptive that even reputable and elite colleges, universities, institutions, and organizations are reducing and even terminating their goodwill efforts to improve DEI in their respective surroundings. See the *Executive Orders* signed by Donald Trump (2020, 2025a, 2025b) to terminate diversity trainings and programs at federal levels.

Like many, I remain confused about the rationale for going against DEI projects and initiatives, especially since they aim to uplift humanity via human valuing, diversity, inclusion, and equanimity (Dukach, 2022; Dunn, 2020; Urwin, 2024; Washington, 2022a, 2022b; Werklabs, 2022). Excitingly, President Joseph Biden (2021) signed the *Executive Order 14035* that supports the principles of *Diversity, Equity, Inclusion, and Accessibility* to dilute the devastations caused by Trump's (2020) retrogressive *Executive Order*. Sadly, there are now visible devastating effects of Trump's (2025a, 2025b) Executive Orders banning DEI. Though I know that no one idea can cure all the ills of our nation, I disagree with the skeptics, cynics, and opponents of DEI projects and initiatives, especially when one considers the multicultural nature of the United States, a nation that consistently prides itself on being the greatest democracy in the world (see Obiakor, 2018, 2020, 2021, 2023b, 2024b). My positional argument is that we must strengthen DEI projects and initiatives to (a) respond to current demographic changes in our society, (b) pursue systemic changes that advance the educational progress of persons from CLD and vulnerable backgrounds, and (c) stabilize concrete ways to build collaborative and productive energies of race, culture, language, national origin, gender, and religion, to mention a few (see Obiakor, 2018, 2020, 2021, 2023b, 2024b).

Educational Implications of DEI Projects

Education has been known to be the great equalizer; and its very essence is to create opportunities for learning and growing. Dewey (1958) rightly posited that education involves growth-oriented experientialism and experimentalism. In other words, education centers on human existence, valuing, and uplift. While this goal of human enhancement is lofty and laudable, people from CLD and vulnerable backgrounds have continued to struggle with traditional ways of learning and teaching in educational programs. As a consequence, they continue to be disenfranchised, disillusioned, disadvantaged, and demeaned and continue to be misidentified, misassessed, mislabeled/miscategorized, misplaced, and misinstructed, making it difficult for them to maximize their fullest potential at all systemic levels (see Obiakor, 2001, 2008, 2018, 2020, 2021, 2023b).

In education (e.g., regular education, special education, and vocational education), critical fields such as Science, Technology, Engineering, and Mathematics and professions such as Medicine and Law, it is imperative that we fully have operational DEI projects and initiatives to achieve the desired goals. There have been some progress in these areas; however, there are many loopholes and vacuums that are yet to be dealt with. While we acknowledge that myriad advocacies, litigations, and legislations have been helpful at different levels, it appears that the fights are not over. Considering the intense traditional and recent hateful struggles about Affirmative Act, race-based admission, book banning in schools and libraries, Black Lives Matter bashing, police brutality and killings, abortion issues, and DEI bashing, we are living in tumultuous hateful times (see Obiakor, 2023b). While there have been efforts to solve these problems, much still deserves to be done. For instance, the Every Student Succeeds Act of 2015 replaced the No Child Left Behind Act to solidify the authenticity of DEI projects and initiatives for elementary and secondary students. And, in special education, the Individuals with Disabilities Education Improvement Act of 2004 reaffirmed the fundamental due process rights of people with disabilities and reenergized great opportunities for (a) student's identification and referral, (b) parental involvement, (c) non-discriminatory assessment, (d) multidisciplinary team, (e) placement in the least restrictive environment, (f) Individualized Education Program, (g) modified instruction, and (h) evaluation. As already indicated, despite these opportunities, learners from CLD and vulnerable backgrounds continue to be misidentified, misassessed, mislabeled/miscategorized, misplaced, and misinstructed. However, these opportunities have created more challenges despite the fact that all educational and socioeconomic processes are rooted in DEI projects and initiatives.

It is critical that we know the make-up of our students, teachers, professors, administrators, staff, and leaders in schools, colleges/universities, institutions, organizations, communities, States, and nation. In fact, a serious and measurable look at these systemic pillars will reveal the ineptness of our thinking and actions toward DEI. In addition, it is important that we mean what we say and say what we mean, especially since we understand the imperative nature of DEI projects and initiatives in our respective fields, professions, and environments. For example, to build the DEI project to maturity in general and special education, we must make frantic and functional efforts at all educational and professional levels. As Washington (2022a, 2022b) proposed, institutions and organizations must become (a) aware, (b) compliant, (c) tactical, (d) integrated, and (e) sustainable. Based on these suggestions, it makes common sense to:

- Create DEI-oriented environments at all educational levels.
- Start early to educate and nurture pre-kindergarten through high school students from CLD and vulnerable backgrounds so that they do not hate school, drop-out, and get into the school-to-prison pipeline.
- Recruit, retain, tenure, and promote pre-kindergarten through high school teachers, principals, and staff who also come from CLD and vulnerable backgrounds to show and give students the hope that people from similar backgrounds can be successful.
- Recruit, retain, reward, acclimatize, and graduate college and university students who come from CLD and vulnerable backgrounds to inspire all students.
- Recruit, retain, tenure, and promote college/university faculty, administrators, and leaders who also come from CLD and vulnerable backgrounds to inspire and motivate undergraduate and graduate students.
- Focus on the needful in building safe spaces and environments, respecting real quality, and cementing DEI projects and initiatives from pre-kindergarten to university levels.

Conclusion

The United States is a multicultural nation that professes to be the greatest democracy in the world; and, efforts to institute DEI projects and initiatives in schools, colleges/universities, and organizations must be appreciated. However, we must acknowledge that DEI projects and initiatives have generated lots of controversies that are not productive and futuristic even though they are operational in our respective homes, institutions, organizations, and communities. Engrained in our human actions are the respect and value of our differences—we must cherish them. While we are witnessing some push-backs on DEI at many educational and institutional levels, we cannot all pretend to "live in a la la land"; we live in a multicultural America, the assumed greatest democracy in the world. So, we must always remember that our future as a nation depends on DEI. To a large extent, we must continue to:

- Experience and experiment new knowledge that will grow the "self" and different "others."

- Shift our paradigms and powers to develop ourselves and communities.
- Incorporate DEI projects and initiatives as we build conscientious communities.
- Enhance human goodness, human valuing, and human progress.
- Elevate avenues for hearing, seeing, feeling, and including different and invisible voices.
- Open more economic, social, and educational doors for *ALL* peoples.

CHAPTER 6

WHY VALUING THE GIFTS AND TALENTS OF MULTICULTURAL PERSONS MATTERS IN EDUCATION AND LIFE

ABSTRACT

The issue of who is gifted or talented has dominated discourses in educational, economic, social, political, athletic, and leadership circles for centuries. More often than not, these discourses exalt people with Whiter skins than people with darker skins. Examples abound that people from culturally and linguistically diverse backgrounds are misidentified, misassessed, mislabeled/miscategorized, misplaced, and miseducated in schools, communities, and institutions. In other words, many human-beings with gifts and talents are devalued, disenfranchised, and disadvantaged because of who they are and where they come from. This chapter focuses on why gifts and talents of multicultural persons matter in education and life.

Keywords: Persons with gifts and talents; understanding intelligences; multicultural persons; enrichment and acceleration programs; innovative strategies; advancing society

Introduction

Over the years, multicultural learners have been systemically misidentified, misassessed, mislabeled/miscategorized, misplaced, and misinstructed; and the wonderful differences that they bring to schools, organizations, institutions, and communities have been frequently downplayed and devalued (Gould, 1981; Obiakor, 2001, 2018, 2020, 2021, 2023b). Many a time, their differences are viewed and interpreted as insurmountable deficits and disadvantages. It is no wonder that schools consistently wrestle with what to do with them. Rather than focus on how to maximize their fullest potential, schools have sometimes looked for the quickest routes to discipline, suspend, and expel them from programs or even send them to prison. As a result, they feel disenfranchised, disadvantaged, disillusioned, and demeaned (see Obiakor, 2018, 2020, 2021, 2023b, 2024a, 2024b; Obiakor et al., 2024). Though I do not object to disciplinary actions against people who are adamantly problematic in schools, organizations, institutions, and communities, it is critical that we challenge systems that focus mostly on punitive deficit-oriented measures instead of remedial and redemption measures.

Our successes as a society have been improperly measured because we continue to devalue the gifts and talents of our citizens who come from culturally and linguistically diverse (CLD) and vulnerable backgrounds. We have failed to focus on functional efforts that can (a) make instructional and educational environments welcoming, and (b) create opportunities to explore the gifts and talents of *ALL* learners. Knowing and seeing the strengths and weaknesses of all human beings is surely good. The problem is that we mostly harp on human weaknesses instead of human strengths. And, we spend more resources looking for weaknesses instead of broadening our horizons and making sure that the gifts and talents that CLD individuals bring to schools, organizations, institutions, and communities are not ignored, downplayed, undervalued, unvalued, underutilized, and unutilized. Should the focus not be on how to help in bringing out the best in *ALL* learners, especially those from CLD and vulnerable backgrounds? This chapter responds to this question and provides ways to innovatively enhance the gifts and talents of CLD individuals.

Contextual Frameworks

Gifts and talents go beyond the walls of culture, race, skin color, religion, national origin, socio-economic status, and personal idiosyncrasy. In practice, we seem to ignore this fundamental knowledge. We make contrary assertions and misidentify, misassess, mislabel/miscategorize, misplace, and miseducate CLD people who are atypically gifted and talented (see Ford & Harris, 1999; Obiakor, 2001; Obiakor et al., 2024). The reality is that we fail ourselves when we fail to understand that our differences are the wonders of our individualities. By not valuing, nurturing, and utilizing the gifts and talents of CLD persons, we victimize them, our institutions, our communities, and our nation as a whole. Additionally, we destroy ourselves as a society when we spend so much money and resources building more jails and prisons instead of funding good redemptive programs and looking for strategies to nurture the gifts and talents of already disenfranchised, disadvantaged, disillusioned, and demeaned CLD and vulnerable populations. It is critical that these populations are (a) provided with fundamental educational and due process rights; (b) valued as different and unique individuals with unique gifts and talents; and (c) provided with curricula that match their learning rates, styles, and complexities.

As noted, the lack of valuing of gifts and talents of CLD persons has been traditional and systemic (Beam, 1980; Cochran & Cotayo, 1983; Dannenberg, 1984; Ford & Harris, 1999; Freehill, 1974). Unfortunately, this continues to be prevalent in today's educational and professional spaces (see Obiakor, 2018, 2020, 2021, 2023a, 2023b; Schlesinger, 1999). Below are cases that buttress this sad reality.

The Case of Maria

Maria was a young brilliant 9th grade Latina who attended a suburban predominantly White high school. She excelled in the sciences (e.g., biology, chemistry, and mathematics). Her dream was to go to a medical school where she would study to become a medical doctor. In Maria's first biology test, she made 100% (i.e., A+ grade) and this got the attention of her teacher and peers. In the second test, she made 100% again; and it became clear that she should be enrolled in advanced biology course. Rather than value, nurture, and enrich her excellent academic performance, the news started going around that she was cheating and copying from her White peers. Maria's parents complained to school authorities; but, there was no seriousness to quell the negative perceptual news. Before long, Maria was frustrated and dropped out of school; and, her parents took her to a new high school where she continued her high school education. This high school had internally well-organized culturally responsive programming. She continued to do well and was put in great enrichment programs. Later, she had a full-ride scholarship to attend a university of her choice. In this university, she was active and successful in her classes even though her White peers were often not pleased that she excelled. Her professors were hesitant and upset to give her the grades that she earned and deserved. When she asked questions in classes, her classmates rolled their eyes in anger. At some point, she stopped asking questions—her professors began to refer to her as arrogant. In one occasion, a classmate got so mad and called her, "an arrogant Mexican bitch who should go back to her country" even though she is a fifth-generation Latina who even struggles to speak her language. She thought about leaving her university and transferring to another college; but, she hung in there to finish her degree. Maria gained admission to a medical school that was not of her choice. In the medical school, she was expecting to have a better and different more mature treatment; but, that was not the case. She began to adjust to negative treatments. She fell sick several times trying to dodge bullets and traps; and in the end, she was successful and went to her Residency in a place of choice. Again, during Residency, the nurses that she worked with frequently disrespected her. Again, she felt like quitting, but hung in there! The struggles were so intense that she fell sick several times; and, her psychological pains were unbearable. In the end, she was successful and landed a job. Some of her colleagues sometimes doubted her based on their facial expressions; but, she had stopped caring about what they thought and continued to do her job in remarkable fashion.

The Case of Madu

Madu was an immigrant Nigerian-born student working on his Ph.D. in a popular Research One University. He was supposed to be the first Black student in his program. He was a great and respectful student with great disposition and zest; and he had a good presence with remarkable social quotient and emotional intelligence. Rather than support, nurture, and enrich his talents, there were measurable plans to expel him because he was dressing up every day and perceived to be arrogant and "too Black" for the program. Specifically, he was not given a graduate assistantship by his department or College; and, the one time he was given, he got one-quarter graduate assistantship. Though he was a good student and writer, he was often viewed as a mediocre writer. Madu was scared—he walked on egg shells and was always dodging all kinds of bullets. Funny enough, he took advantage of his experiences as an English language high school teacher to assist his peers in their writing skills (e.g., he edited and sometimes rewrote their works). Madu continued to advance in his Ph.D. program; and, many of his peers were dropping and failing out—he became one of the fittest that survived. Because of the high reputation of the program, many of his doctoral peers were offered jobs in very reputable colleges and universities. However, he had difficulty getting a job while his less qualified peers were landing excellent job opportunities. He finally landed his first job in a small historically Black college and university (HBCU) and made the best of it before moving to bigger and more reputable universities. As the years passed, he became one of the national/international leaders in his field and areas of interest. He became nationally and internationally known for his teaching, scholarship, service, leadership, visibility, and professional activities. Madu excelled as a teacher, scholar, and professional; and, he mentored his colleagues on and off campuses. In his department, he was ranked highly in end-of-year evaluations and earned exceptional merits. Despite his accomplishments, getting tenure or promotion was always dramatic and sometimes hilarious—his accent, teaching, and arrogance were always in play; yet, his less competent colleagues who he mentored were tenured and promoted with ease and zero drama. The goals of his colleagues were for him to be invisible and silent. Before long, he was assigned to coordinate and direct departmental programs. His jobs as program coordinator and director were very difficult to manage and handle—everyone took credit when there was success. But, he was always to blame for everything when problems and failures came up. Despite all his career achievements, he continued to endure racism, xenophobia, discrimination, and hatred. In fact, the same White colleagues who he mentored and supported to gain tenure and promotion frequently ganged up against him since he was typically the only Black male professor. The "ganging up" behavior intensified when the news started going around that he would like to be the department head. Everything and the kitchen sink were thrown at him—the worst and most potent of them was sexual harassment. Who was to defend the lonely immigrant Black man from Nigeria? Sadly, he was on his own! Madu eventually landed and accepted a job as department head elsewhere. But, the troubles of this immigrant Black man were not over. On two separate universities, he served as department head. In both cases, he increased the rankings of all programs in his departments; and, he got them through all state and national accreditations. Even as a leader, he continued to excel in his teaching, scholarly, and professional activities. Consequently, Madu was invited to apply for deanship positions; and with trepidation, he ventured out to achieve the deanship goal. He had more than 150 telephone/skype interviews and went to 50 plus campus visits as one of the top candidates. And, he never landed a notable position—the only one he landed offered him a very low salary which offerors knew that he would easily reject.

To many skeptical minds, Cases of Maria and Madu might be unreal, accidental, unique, and less frequent. Unfortunately, Cases like them happen frequently and with intensity. While it is easy to engage in rationalizations and debates about "what is" or "what is not," the fact remains that Maria and Madu are human beings who deserve some humane treatments. They were hurt when their gifts and talents were not valued, nurtured, and utilized. This logically means that when human beings are diminished, silenced, and made invisible, their spirits and aspirations are dampened, destroyed, or even killed. As a consequence, all human beings, including CLD students with gifts and talents must be supported and inspired to be their best by their organizations, institutions, communities, nation, and world. When we do the needful, we all immensely gain!

Multicultural Persons With Gifts and Talents: Who They Are

People with gifts and talents have abilities that affect a broad spectrum of their lives—these abilities include thinking, creativity, and leadership, to mention a few. These individuals usually (a) demonstrate curiosity about new ideas, (b) seek answers inquisitively, (c) solve problems in unusual ways, and (d) engage in outside-the-box strategies. As students, they are identified in grades 1–12 as demonstrating high performance ability or potential in academic and/or artistic areas and therefore require an educational program beyond what is normally provided by general school programs to achieve their potential (Hansford, 1985; Kaplan, 2005). Programming for these students must include a variety of options, including acceleration, enrichment, in-depth work in selected areas of study, and opportunities for community-based and "beyond the classroom" learning through mentorships and summer and weekend programs. Some of the needs of these students can be met in regular classrooms with adequate teacher training and support services. Teachers and related professionals who work with these learners must be carefully selected and trained in gifted education; and their curriculum must be designed to be rigorous, deep, and complex.

Clearly, 21st century education must reflect 21st century thinking. All hands must be on deck in looking for new ways of doing things. Different students require different education! In other words, instruction must be differently tiered to meet the needs of students with gifts and talents. *Differentiation* is a broad term that refers to the need to tailor teaching environments, curricula, and instructional practices to create appropriately different learning experiences for students with different needs, interests, readiness, and learning profiles (Tomlinson, 1999, 2005, 2011). The reality that gifted learners differ in meaningful ways is the guiding premise of differentiation. The main objective is to engage learners in instruction through different learning modalities, appealing to differing interests, using varied rates of instruction, and providing varied degrees of complexity within and across a challenging and conceptually rich curriculum. Meaningful curriculum differentiation for students with gifts and talents requires that educators and service providers recognize individual strengths of these learners and acknowledge the inadequacy of the regular curriculum to meet those needs (Kaplan, 2005; Tomlinson, 1999, 2005, 2011). For example, gifted and talented programs include skipping grades, early entrance, early graduation, credit by examination, non-graded classes, and advanced placement classes. Some students with gifts and talents who seem bored in school may benefit from accelerated programs that provide academic challenges and keep them involved in school.

It is important to know that giftedness does not lie so much in the possession of a certain number of traits; it lies in the degree and combinations in which some of the traits may be present. When a high degree of curiosity is present, in combination with resourcefulness, perseverance, and a drive to organize and perfect, it may take the form of an intense desire to probe until a solution has been found and may well be an indication of giftedness. For example, a student may be failing to make good grades in school; however, this same student can dislodge a computer and put it together. Most of the society's technological gurus are college and university drop-outs who are today's billionaires. A logical extension is that many CLD learners may excel beyond bounds if and when they are given opportunities to be creative, that is, not using one modality to assess their gifts and talents.

More than three decades ago, Howard Gardner (1993) in his *Model of Multiple Intelligences* identified seven intelligences, namely:

- Musical intelligence.
- Bodily-kinesthetic intelligence.
- Logical mathematical intelligence.

- Linguistic intelligence.
- Spatial intelligence.
- Interpersonal intelligence.
- Intrapersonal intelligence.

Gardner's (1993) goal was to reiterate the phenomena of human differences and human intelligences. This model harps on instructional differentiation that represents the heart of the individualized education programs in general and special education. Additionally, it challenges educators and service providers to know their students, and design programs that value their capabilities and strengths. Of late, the number of intelligences has been expanded to include spiritual intelligence, naturalistic intelligence, and existential intelligence. But, without dabbling into deeper explanations, the message is clear—intelligences are multidimensional and go beyond race, language, gender, skin color, religion, national origin, personal idiosyncrasies, and so on. Three critical questions then come to mind. Why do schools, colleges/universities, institutions, and organizations continue to use units of scores or grades to judge our intelligence quotient or how intelligent we are? Why are we not seriously interrogating the fact that the intelligences of many learners, especially those from CLD and vulnerable populations, are not been properly assessed and nurtured? And, why are we not worried that our fellow humans are allowed to fall through the cracks because their gifts and talents are not valued and grown?

Moving Forward

We now know that efforts to provide gifted and talented CLD students with equitable educational opportunities have been inundated with problems, despite the range of educational programming and service delivery options (e.g., enrichment, acceleration, mentoring, cluster programs, pull-out programs, special classes, ability grouping, and combination programs). For some reason, most teachers and school administrators have very little or no training in meeting the unique learning needs of their students. Sadly, many of the existing programs do not infuse critical elements (e.g., culturally responsive teaching) that provide for the individual needs of students with gifts and talents. Moving forward, something has to change!

It is critical that we value and nurture all multicultural persons, especially those with gifts and talents. Gardner (1993) suggested that very early, "in the preschool and early elementary years, instruction should emphasize opportunity. It is during these years that children can discover something of their own peculiar interests and abilities" (p. 29). Clearly, not valuing and nurturing children and youth handicaps them and also handicaps their schools, communities, institutions, organizations, and nation. *This is synonymous with a track star preparing for the Olympic game and takes a gun to shoot and damage his/her two legs; and yet, he/she still wants or is expected to win the race. That will never be possible!* If we want to advance our society and nation, we must take advantage of the gifts and talents of every one of our citizens. In consonance, we must shift our paradigms and powers in ways that we judge and perceive people who are different. And, when they are different by race, color, national origin, religion, and personal idiosyncrasy, we have the obligation to respect, value, and nurture them. It is also our duty to give them the opportunities to grow and become the best that they can be. If we do not, we will be inflicting personal and emotional injuries on them while also short-selling them and our society. Our purpose for schooling our children and youth should not be to injure or short-sell them; it should be to develop, nurture, enrich, and uplift them. As Gardner (1993) rightly pointed out:

> The purpose of school should be to develop intelligences and to help people reach vocational and avocational goals that are appropriate to their particular spectrum of intelligences. People who are helped to do so, I believe, feel more engaged and competent, and therefore more inclined to serve the society in a constructive way. (p. 9)

Conclusion

Somehow, we seem to have forgotten the goals of education and the society. In our search for quality, we seem to have lost our direction. In education, we typically acknowledge individual differences; yet, we fail to practice it in our instructional models. Very often, we treat every child and youth as the same and grade them as the same. In reality, we are all different, and that is the wonder of our individualities. Many of our students with gifts and talents are slipping through the cracks—we are not nurturing them the ways we should, especially when they come from CLD and vulnerable backgrounds. As a result, we must make systemic changes in our educational practices, socio-economic strategies, and political thinking. We need to prepare teachers and related professionals to maximize the potential of students with gifts and talents, despite their backgrounds. As facilitators of learning, we must seek to improve educational practices in schools, raise the base level of expectations for all, and allow students with gifts and talents to go beyond imaginations to reach their potential. We must appreciate the fact that these students perform at high levels when they receive instruction under a qualified or certified teacher. We do not need teachers and service providers who lack a repertoire of practical ideas, strategies, and techniques within a diverse classroom. Additionally, we do not need professionals who are inept in their interpretation of affective, social, emotional, psychological, and motivational needs of students with gifts and talents. This ineptness must not be allowed to exist in a society or schooling environment that plans to compete in our global economy. This means that Educator Preparation Programs must play crucial roles in preparing teachers and service providers to maximize the potential of *ALL* students. Finally, more than ever, it is imperative that all educational programs and services do whatever it takes to provide appropriate enrichment programs for *ALL* students, especially those from CLD and vulnerable backgrounds. In the classic words of Gardner (1993):

> It is of the utmost importance that we recognize and nurture all of the varied human intelligences and all of the combinations of intelligences. We are all so different largely because we all have different combinations of intelligences. If we recognize this, I think we will have at least a better chance of dealing appropriately with the many problems that we face in the world. If we can mobilize the spectrum of human abilities, not only will people feel better about themselves and more competent; it is even possible that they will also feel more engaged and better able to join the rest of the world community in working for the broader good. Perhaps if we can mobilize the full range of human intelligences and ally them to an ethical sense, we can help to increase the likelihood of our survival on this planet, and perhaps even contribute to our thriving. (p. 12)

CHAPTER 7

WHY VOICES OF STUDENTS FROM CULTURALLY AND LINGUISTICALLY DIVERSE BACKGROUNDS MATTER IN EDUCATION

ABSTRACT

No brain is a tabula rasa (i.e., blank slate). This statement means that all human-beings, in this case, students have voices and ideas about their personal well-being and situations. Sadly, in education, this is not usually the case. By their actions, some general and special educational professionals tend to silent voices of their students and families by treating them unprofessionally, unethically, and soullessly. These negative and sometimes hateful behaviors are more visible when they work with students from culturally and linguistically diverse (CLD) backgrounds. For example, they fail to listen to students and their parents and give these students more time-outs, suspensions, and expulsions than their White classmates. In reality, these CLD students should be valued, respected, and involved just like other students. This chapter addresses why voices of CLD students matter at all educational levels.

Keywords: Voices of students; CLD students; general and special education; professional and ethical behaviors; educational success; growing the future

Introduction

Have you ever gone to a medical doctor for diagnosis of some illness without being asked how you are feeling or where it hurts? Will you like the doctor to prescribe medication or treatment immediately without knowing what is wrong with you? Only a quack doctor can do that! Based on personal experiences, most, if not all medical doctors like to hear your voice before prescribing any medical treatment. This logically means that your voice matters whenever you go to your doctor. In education, especially in special education, the scenarios are different. More often than not, *we see teachers and other related professionals prescribe remediation based on the information from the student's file or based on their experience with one unique student in a unique class under a unique situation.* As a result, they engage in anti-teaching behaviors that include:

- Teaching and leading students who they do not really know.
- Making judgments about students and even disciplining them without putting them to the test.
- Using tools that lack reliability and validity to test students.
- Disproportionately placing students in inappropriate programs.
- Leaving students to rot in programs that do not match their talents and abilities.
- Getting surprised that students are dropping out of school or getting entangled in the web of school-to-prison pipeline.
- Pretending that racism is over and operating from the framework of that thinking.

Why do educators and related professionals engage in the aforementioned anti-teaching behaviors? Is it not important that we continue to interrogate why it is difficult for educators to (a) understand that voices of students are important in their educational processes; and (b) challenge and discipline their own professional equilibrium? My guess is there are no repercussions for their actions!

It is time that we challenged the normalization of certain abnormal behaviors by professionals in school activities and programs. We must continue to wonder why it is normal for educators and service providers to (a) label students, (b) dump all kinds of negative information about them in their folders, (c) spread negative information about them in the *faculty lounge,* and (d) convince colleagues to see the negativism that we saw in students in specific programs. Unfortunately, these professional abnormal behaviors cause tremendous harm to students from CLD and vulnerable backgrounds experience as they interact with school programs. And, these abnormalities make it imperative to make sure that (a) voices of CLD learners are heard and not silenced in school programs, and (b) vulnerable students are assisted in maximizing their learning and life potentials in educational and life journeys. These are the foci of this chapter.

Contextual Frameworks

It is now common knowledge that racism, xenophobia, linguistic bigotry, and religious dogmatism exist in our communities. Not questioning the existence of these problems in our social fabric is mere foolery; and giving up on tackling them is even more foolery. We cannot fake solutions to these problems anymore; we can no longer sweep them under the rug; and we cannot give up in interrogating our failures to tackle them (see Obiakor, 2018, 2020, 2021, 2023a, 2023b). We must begin to understand that these problems are experienced by fellow human beings who live amongst us. The concerns of different "others" are the concerns of all, and vice versa. From pre-kindergarten to university levels, voices of CLD and vulnerable students are important and critical. Silencing these voices or making people who have these voices to be invisible is anti-education and anti-humanity.

Apparently, many teachers and related professionals find it difficult to accept that they silent different voices in their classrooms and programs. In reality, they do! Diangelo (2022), in her book, *Nice Racism: How Progressive White People Perpetuate Racial Harm*, presented intricate societal nuances that manifest themselves in racial interactions. As Diangelo (2022) noted, though well-intentioned, some White people are so uneasy about racism that they act very strange; and, their actions include:

- Engaging in patronizing or paternalistic behaviors.
- Overcompensating on trivial racial matters.
- Rushing to prove that they are not racist.
- Downplaying White advantage.
- Pretending that White racism simply happens.
- Making weird statements like, "I know what you are going through" or "I have a minority friend."
- Assuming that racism only happens to "poor" or "uneducated" people.
- Reminding people that they have traveled far and wide.
- Believing in blind equality.
- Professing to know more than they know.
- Feeling destroyed by shame.

These intricate nuances may not be intentional; but, they show "little learning" that may be harmful and counter-productive to CLD learners, their families, and their communities (read Alexander Pope's 1711 work, *An Essay on Criticism*). In his work, Pope (1711) elucidated the dangerous ramifications of "little learning" in any society. I posit that it is a sign of little learning to silence voices of already disenfranchised, disadvantaged, disillusioned, and demeaned people. How do we know them and their pains? And, how do we know what motivates and inspires them? Sadly, even when we attempt to listen to them, we presume that we are doing them a favor. By so doing, we belittle what they think, mean, see, hear, feel, say, and do.

Hearing Culturally Relevant Voices on School Campuses

Many interesting and non-interesting things happen in the four walls of school campuses. While I believe in the sanctity of these walls, we must pay serious attention to the happenings inside them. The reason is simple: *OUR FUTURE AS A SOCIETY DEPENDS ON IT!* Our children and family members operate within these four walls; and, it is imperative that we hear their voices. Let's look briefly into the voices of students inside these walls from pre-kindergarten to university levels below.

Pre-Kindergarten and Kindergarten Programs

In pre-kindergarten and kindergarten programs are children who are not very excited to leave home for their new learning environments. These children cry a lot as they get used to these environments. So, the initial goal should be to get excited about going to school. To achieve this goal, their young voices should be heard—this means that teachers and related professionals should work hand-in-glove with families/parents to understand their likes and dislikes. At these levels, such collaborative activities are important to CLD students and their families (Obiakor, 2001, 2008; Obiakor et al., 2024). Assignments should be age-appropriate and should allow students to share their voices through their drawings, art works, stories, and songs. To buttress early and healthy learning environments, constructivist classrooms must be instituted to reduce the linearity and increase the multidimensionality in educational processes (Grennon Brooks & Brooks, 2001). In addition, students' perspectives of their works must be shared and discussed from socio-cultural and linguistic lenses (see Obiakor et al., 2024). Finally, relationships, interactions, games, and plays must be encouraged and advanced in all instructional activities to entice young learners.

Elementary School Programs

Inside the walls of elementary classrooms, young students are worried about their new environments (e.g., who is sitting around them, who they like or dislike, and what teachers and service providers are like, especially when they raise their hands to answer questions). Not hearing them and not taking them seriously might create some uneasiness in them. Many students from CLD and vulnerable backgrounds find mainstream school environments to be strange and unwelcoming (Obiakor, 2001, 2007, 2008, 2018, 2020, 2021, 2023b, 2024b; Obiakor et al., 2024). It is critical that they are allowed to share who they are, what they like or dislike, what their homes are like, and what their aspirations are to mention a few. At this level, CLD students should participate in developing friendships that carry over to field trips, co-curricular activities, recreational activities, and so on.

Middle School Programs

Inside the walls of middle schools, students who are now teenagers start talking about relationships, boyfriends, and girlfriends; and they participate in activities that they like (e.g., going camping). In middle schools, CLD students begin to truly experience exclusion in some social activities; and they pay attention to how students and teachers interact with them during classroom discussions. Ignoring their voices at home and in schools can lead to depression and other psychological problems (e.g., school drop-out and drug abuse). Many CLD and vulnerable students are rarely seen or heard; and, they fall into the traps of disenfranchisements and disruptions in their school activities (Obiakor, 2001, 2007, 2008, 2018, 2020, 2021, 2024b; Obiakor et al., 2024). It is critical that school personnel and leaders (e.g., counselors and therapists) create crisis intervention programs to remediate teenage problems that students confront in middle school programs. In addition, to hear students' voices, they must be assured that they are worthy members of the school community; and, safe spaces must be created to reduce their at-risk and vulnerable situations.

High School Programs

Inside the walls of high schools, students are faced with performing well academically to prepare for college admission, high school graduation, and teenage-to-adulthood stages. As a result of these stressors, some of them resort to dropping out, drug dealing and taking, and engaging in antisocial behaviors that lead to school-to-prison pipeline. Many CLD and vulnerable students confront similar problems, but with great intensity. This means that teachers and school personnel (e.g., counselors, therapists, special educators, principals, and superintendents) need to hear from students to know the stressors that they are under. By creating such opportunities to talk, students use their voices to advocate for themselves. This is the more reason why all stakeholders must actively listen, intentionally learn, and seriously act in ways that are caring and culturally responsive to students (see Obiakor, 2001, 2007, 2008, 2018; Obiakor et al., 2024).

College/University Campuses

Inside the four walls of college/university campuses, students find themselves in new environments and try to find their ways out of the mazes that confront them. On campus, for many CLD students, they see few role models, teachers, staff, administrators, and leaders who look like them; and they quietly question why situations are that way. As examples show, they go to cafeterias and see students sitting together according to race and skin color. In their classes, they see zero or few students or professors who look like them. In addition, they go to football and basketball games and see players who look like them and coaches who do not like them. Over all, they see staff, administrators, and leaders who do not look like them. These White dominated environments make life for CLD students to be lonely and scary (see Obiakor, 2020, 2021, 2021, 2023b, 2024b). It is no wonder that these students feel worried when they see that the campus DEI offices that are supposed to protect them are being threatened and closed. Considering all these barriers confronting CLD students, it is literally dangerous to silence their voices and not know how they are surviving on campus. It is beneficial to them, their families, and their colleges/universities to hear their stories. Clearly, students at undergraduate, graduate, post-graduate, and professional degree levels must be seen and heard—their voices are critically needed to add realities to campus life, health, and sanity.

Conclusion

It is clear that all students, including CLD students have unique experiences that require unique attention. As indicated, at all educational levels, CLD students experience visible and invisible racism, xenophobia, and discriminatory actions that lead to disenfranchisements, disadvantages, and disillusionments. To deal with these problems and situations, we must make dedicated efforts to *hear their voices*. In addition, we must create avenues and spaces for them to (a) speak truth to power, (b) tell their stories, (c) go beyond their comfort zones, (d) analyze problems, and (e) find solutions collaboratively, consultatively, and cooperatively. It is time that we realized that CLD students are lonely, silenced, and demeaned in predominantly White campuses, institutions, and organizations. In addition, we must realize that they suffer emotionally, academically, psychologically, and socially when they feel estranged. All of these problems make it imperative for educational institutions and community organizations to (a) make frantic and functional efforts to hear the voices of CLD students at all levels, (b) institute and solidify DEI programs at all educational levels, and (c) make measurable culturally responsive changes that can advance our overall educational, economic, political, and social systems.

CHAPTER 8

WHY VOICES OF FAMILIES FROM CULTURALLY AND LINGUISTICALLY DIVERSE BACKGROUNDS MATTER IN EDUCATION

ABSTRACT

Families are critical in the lives of children—they play central roles in the education and growth of their children. They know the strengths, weaknesses, and dispositions of their children; and, they are always willing to be involved on issues concerning their children. In some educational quarters, they are ignored and treated without respect and value, especially when they come from culturally and linguistically diverse (CLD) backgrounds. In addition, they are blamed for their children's problems and disenfranchised in educational programming. For parents whose children have special needs, their voices are sometimes ignored in designing individualized education programs (IEPs) even though they are supposed to be active participants in the system. The fact remains that without parental voices, students' educational successes are directly or indirectly delayed and stunted. This chapter focuses on why voices of families from CLD backgrounds matter in education and communities.

Keywords: Voices of families; CLD families; parental rights; collaborating and consulting with parents; empowering parents; advancing communities

Introduction

It is always easy to credit or blame families when things go right or wrong; yet, they are either over wanted or not wanted at all in educational programs. At times, practitioners and leaders lose their minds when it comes to parents and families from CLD and vulnerable backgrounds. Typically, assumptions, labels, and categories related to racism and discriminatory practices run wild about these families. It is no wonder that they are frequently disadvantaged, disillusioned, and demeaned. About 50 years ago, Gordon (1975) put it succinctly:

> Everybody blames parents for the troubles of youth and for the troubles that young people appear to be causing society. It's all the fault of parents, mental health experts lament, after examining the frightening statistics on the rapidly increasing number and youth who develop serious and crippling emotional problems, who become victims of drug addiction, or commit suicide. Political leaders and law-enforcement officials blame parents for raising a generation of ingrates, rebels, protesters, hippies, peace demonstrators, and draft-card burners. And when kids fail in school or become hopeless drop-outs, teachers and school administrators claim that the parents are at fault. (p. 1)

Based on the notations above, similar issues and problems have continued to take place today. It is sad that parents, especially those from CLD and vulnerable backgrounds are bombarded with blames when things go wrong with their children. Consistently, parents who are financially "poor" are defined by the "poor" construct—they are categorized as having "poor" self-concepts, "poor" morals, "poor" self-responsibility, and "poor" brains to do anything; and they are presumed to live in "poor" communities. On the other hand, parents who are financially and economically wealthy and viable are perceived to be "great" parents who function with "great" brains and live in "great" communities. The question continues to be, Where are the voices of families in education today? Yes, we hear *some* voices and not *all* voices; and some of them have been counter-productive, disingenuous, and even repugnant. Rather than become voices of reason and change, some of them have become enemies of change, particularly when they engage in xenophobic, racist, and discriminatory actions that destroy bridges that unite humanity. For instance, some of them have been responsible for banning books and excluding students who they deem to be atypical. Though I object to venomous parental voices, I believe more voices are better than no voice at all (Obiakor, 2018, 2020, 2021, 2023b). It is critical that we encourage more productive voices that lead to constructive actions. This means that we need to hear voices of CLD families/parents to enhance and market creative programming, equitable and open-minded education, and human valuing and progress. This is the central focus of this chapter.

Human Valuing and Family Voices

Human beings are similar and different. While they want to be appreciated and valued, they also want to be unique for who they are—this uniqueness makes them different and their differences are reflected in their values. Logically, value systems influence their human perceptions and relationships; and these relationships expose strange problems and realities of our human existence. All of these variables lead to false prophecy and fraudulent multiculturalism—these occur when people pretend to know more than they know or less than they know. Though some relationships can be phony, most relationships have good intentions and can sometimes lead to real solutions to real problems that affect real lives. And, when these human problems intensify, people's differences, beliefs, cultures, languages, religions, national origins, and genders collide (Beachum & McCray, 2011). Additionally, when collusions occur, people get hurt and everyone loses (Obiakor, 2023b).

It is common knowledge that human perceptions affect human valuations that may be right or wrong. This is true for students, families, and communities, particularly those from CLD and vulnerable backgrounds. As Kroth and Edge (1997) explained about three decades ago,

> Many factors influence one's perceptions, the quality of a parent-teacher interaction, the process, and ultimately the outcome. Each participant brings to the exchange certain physical, emotional, and behavioral characteristics and past history, which all affect the individual's perception of the world. These characteristics are considered *inputs*, and they have potential effect on all interactions. In some cases these characteristics generate such strong feelings that two individuals may not be able to enter into a working relationship. One of the major factors affecting the parent-teacher relationship is the value system of each of the participants. (p. 68)

As humans, we consistently judge others and make attributions about them, correctly or incorrectly. Cyclically, others who hear us get biased and join us in judging them, correctly or incorrectly. And, by judging others, we give the impression that we are better than them, sometimes for no reason. Kroth and Edge (1997) correctly noted that "the better one understands one's own and others' value systems, the fewer judgments one is likely to make about apparent inconsistencies in behavior" (p. 69).

Clearly, the hypocrisy of human judgments is always sad, intriguing, and sometimes funny. We consistently see people who profess to have high moral compass exhibit behaviors that are below board. Sometimes, we rationalize their awful behaviors if they suit our personal idiosyncrasies. For example, not long ago, Walker (2023) reported that Mrs. Bridget Ziegler (the co-founder of *Moms for Liberty*) and her husband who profess to be moral giants were involved in several deviant sex scandals. Mrs. Ziegler who was serving as a Sarasota County School Board member was asked to resign. For clarity, the *Moms for Liberty* group is an extremely aggressive conservative Christian fundamentalist group that consistently made very racist, homophobic, and discriminatory pronouncements about public school students, teachers, administrators, and curricula. While I am not suggesting that we police people's moralities and judgments or punish people for making discriminatory pronouncements, I am saying that we must be (a) vigilant about people's moral compass, and (b) careful about prejudicial judgments and pronouncements. The reason is that prejudicial judgments hurt and destroy human beings (Obiakor, 2023b). Even when judgments are correct, they can overrate who we are, thereby constituting another major psychological problem. Consider this example—*when we assume that a mediocre and hateful White teacher who teaches students with gifts and talents is also gifted, it creates the problem of exalting false prophesy and White supremacy.* I have strong belief that teaching students with gifts and talents does not automatically mean that the teacher is gifted or talented.

Many a time, on issues of hypocrisy, parental values, and teacher behaviors, we are obligated to ask questions. Unfortunately, we sometimes refuse or feel hesitant to ask important questions. My hunch is that it is in our favor to ask, What values should we adopt or emulate in educational processes? What defines and constitutes a good parent or good parenting in education? And, what parental voices matter in educational interactions? Without asking these questions, it is a fool's paradise to expect up-to-date answers that are relevant to our mutual interactions. It is our responsibility to (a) value the voices of families that are different racially, culturally, linguistically, religiously, and nationally; (b) respect *ALL* families as they communicate with educators and related professionals; and (c) build mutual relationships that buttress educational goals (Barnlund, 1976; Kroth & Edge, 1997). For example, Kroth and Edge (1997) acknowledged that

> ... many parents feel lost in the maze of educating children. Some do not have support systems—family members, schools, and community agencies. They fear the system and what it may do to their children if they complain. They don't know how to access the systems and how to get services. (p. 19)

This means that voices of families must be taken seriously. For many families from CLD and vulnerable families, their voices must not be silenced—they must be heard in visible ways. These families have unique experiences and perspectives that are useful and meaningful in the education of their children and family members. We cannot build relationships in a vacuum—we must know these parents, their values, and their communities. Making prejudicial assumptions about them is dangerous, unproductive, anti-education, and anti-humanity.

Future Perspectives

As rough as situations appear sometimes, the future is not usually as dark as it may seem. Usually, mistakes are made and people learn from them. Families are no different! One thing is clear—families have the prime responsibility to always advocate for their loved ones. Sadly, voices of families from CLD and vulnerable backgrounds are not properly received in educational quarters. As it appears, when they complain, we view them as "trouble makers," "noise makers," and "bad"; and when they do not complain and allow teachers and related professionals to do what is right, we view them as "nonchalant," "uneducated," and "ignorant." On the other hand, when White parents complain, we view them as "involved," "serious" and "good"; and when they do not get involved, we view them as "busy," "professional," and "stressed." It sounds like CLD and vulnerable parents/families cannot win—everything about them is viewed from negative and deficit perspectives; and everything about White parents/families is viewed from positive and strength-based perspectives. For education to do what it is supposed to do (i.e., educate, value and grow people), we must educate all people and value all voices, even if they seem unattractive.

In the future, we must make efforts to shift our paradigms and powers on how we work with parents and families, particularly those from CLD and vulnerable backgrounds. Just as we value ourselves, we must value others who are different from us. Gordon (1975) urged school personnel to train families/parents in what he called *Parent Effectiveness Training*; however, I have always been worried about cultures, languages, and values to be used during such trainings. It is not realistic to give people trainings that are loaded with prejudice and White supremacy. Instead of trainings, I suggest "hearty" meetings and conversations that treat participants as equal partners in order to stimulate the willingness to share ideas (Obiakor, 2018). Again, blaming or labeling families/parents instead of collaboratively, consultatively, and cooperatively working with them is disastrous. For example, in drug abuse situations, they can be very instrumental in remediating or solving the problem by serving as contact persons, resource persons, and informants to schools and respective authorities (Obiakor, 2008; Obiakor et al., 1997; Wilmes, 1988). Earlier, Barnlund (1976) reminded educators and related professionals to be sensitive to egos, differences, social strata, communication styles, and personal idiosyncrasies to get maximum participation from families/parents. It is imperative that we know why CLD and vulnerable families/parents are hesitant to be involved in what schools do. Kroth and Edge (1997) further suggested that school personnel and leaders change their perspectives on (a) time, (b) intimidation, (c) systemic understanding, (d) child care, (e) language, (f) culture, (g) transportation, and (h) comfortability. As an example, White people and different "others" differ on their views on time. As a young man in Nigeria, my father told me not to allow time to control me, that is, that I should always control my time. In the United States, I learned that time is a very serious phenomenon that controls most events. While they might sound alike, my experiences in the United States have helped me to see the differences. Strangely, I have never been in a hurry about time; yet, I have always been in a hurry to meet timelines and deadlines. So, when friends invite me to occasions or when I invite them to occasions, I have learned to balance situations. We need to understand that cultures, languages, and values infiltrate into whatever we do—this means that it is dangerous to misjudge and mislabel/miscategorize families/parents who we know nothing or little about.

It is critical that we enrich our school environments to make them more productive and service-oriented to communities. Rather than silence voices, we should use families/parents as consultants, resource persons, co-teachers, and co-counselors, as needed. In addition, we should take advantage of the wealth of knowledge and information that they have and get them empowered as we interact with them. The reason is that *THEY KNOW THEIR CHILDREN!* This means that looking down on them does not in any way favor schools and those who work in them. Instead of hating or competing with them, we must see them as our equal partners today, tomorrow, and forever.

Conclusion

This chapter reaffirms that voices of families/parents are necessary to maximize their fullest potential as equal participants with educators, related professionals, and service providers. All families/parents matter, including those from CLD and vulnerable backgrounds. We cannot ignore and silent these voices in the education of their children. To a large measure, all stakeholders are critical elements in the educational processes of young children and youth. As a result, we have to be sensitive to their cultures, languages, values, communication styles, and personal idiosyncrasies. In addition, we must care about others who are different and unique—their differences and uniqueness are their beauties.

Finally, we must all agree that downplaying, demeaning, and devaluing CLD families/parents are extremely costly to programs, schools, and communities—not only do they know their children, they also can be informants and resource persons on critical issues. As Kroth and Edge (1997) concluded:

> Considering the vast changes in families and the risk of failure placed on children in our society, one easily could lose hope for children having a better chance for survival and success in life. To bring the dreams for our nation's children to fruition, better policies for parent/family involvement in education have to be developed, along with more opportunities for children to gain full support from families, schools, and community agencies. (p. 21)

CHAPTER 9

WHY COMMUNITY VOICES MATTER IN MULTICULTURAL EDUCATION AND INTERACTIONS

ABSTRACT

Communities are central hubs of human habitations; and facilities that fortify human existence are located in them. Examples include schools, colleges, universities, businesses, institutions, organizations, churches, temples, and mosques. All of these make life worth living for students, families, and other stakeholders. As a result, it is critical that community voices are heard in situations that concern them. However, community voices of people from culturally and linguistically diverse (CLD) backgrounds are frequently silenced and disregarded because of racial, socioeconomic, and political divides. Without hearing ALL voices, societal perennial problems will remain unsolved, thereby causing more disruptions, disasters, and deaths. It is no surprise that educational and other accrediting agencies are interested in hearing community voices to solve critical problems. This chapter discusses why community voices matter in multicultural education and interactions.

Keywords: Communities; community voices; CLD communities; students and parents; schools and institutions; societal advancement

Introduction

Everywhere in the world, we hear so much about communities; but, there is always a presumption of innocence about them. In earnest, very few questions are asked about them. In this chapter, I ask critical community-related questions that deserve some answers and reiterate the importance of community voices in building schools. Who makes up a community? What makes up a good community? Why do institutions and organizations try to know the goings-on in communities? Why do businesses study what communities think about them and their products? Why do school and university accrediting bodies try to get the views and perspectives of community members? Why are community voices critical at all levels of our society? Why do schools, colleges, universities, institutions, and organizations appoint people to be their community representatives and liaisons? And, specifically, why is it necessary to hear voices of people from CLD and vulnerable backgrounds in communities? These are important questions that seem to be ignored (but should not be ignored) by those who profess to own and run communities. There is the tendency to forget that people, educational institutions, businesses, churches, synagogues, mosques, and organizations make up communities. Typically, these community entities analyze, evaluate, and appreciate communities before locating in them; and they make their voices heard in discourses regarding economic, political, educational, and societal advancements. In unsafe, divided, dis-oriented, and hateful communities, pillars of society (e.g., families, churches, synagogues, businesses, and organizations) relocate to find safer, more unified, better-oriented, and loving communities (Obiakor, 2023b; Obiakor et al., 2002). This is why we must continuously ask, Why are community voices important? What can be done to encourage and nurture these voices, particularly those of people from CLD and vulnerable backgrounds? How can we take advantage of such voices to advance our students, families, schools, communities, and government entities? In reality, answering these thought-provoking questions will help to revamp, rebuild, and grow our communities and other entities that are located in them.

Contextualizing Communities

Communities have their own cultures and values; but, they do not exist or grow in isolation (Dooley & Toscano-Nixon, 2002; Obiakor et al., 2002). Traditionally, communities are narrowly defined as either "good" or "bad." As noted earlier, "good" communities are translated as where the "rich" people live and "bad" communities are translated mostly as where the "poor" people live. As also noted earlier, these explanations are based on presumptive perceptions. Dooley and Toscano-Nixon (2002) explained a community as:

> A society of people having common rights and privileges, or common interests, civil, and political, and living under the same laws and regulations. Because of the heterogeneous nature of the society, there are different types of communities. Communities take on many different forms and often times, social, political, cultural, economic norms, and/or values influence the capacity of the community. (p. 99)

Frequently, communities provide comprehensive opportunities to solve all kinds of problems to meet the needs of all people, including CLD and vulnerable children, youth, and families. Communities usually work together to build and reform their communities; and they cannot be good communities if they ignore their children, youth, adults, families, teachers, schools, to mention a few. To fully understand communities, we must properly contextualize them.

There are communities that are:

- *Dysfunctional and Struggling Communities*—these are communities where there is zero to little involvement in development and accountability processes.
- *Borderline Communities*—these are communities with minimum participation that rely more on governments to impose changes.
- *Conscientious Communities*—these are communities where people participate in words and actions with common goal-directed purpose.

It is important to save and work with dysfunctional and struggling and borderline communities. We cannot afford to allow them to decay. But, if we do not work hard to sustain conscientious communities, they will decline, struggle, and be dysfunctional. Arllen et al. (1997) and Obiakor (2018, 2020, 2021, 2023b) argued that the goal is always to produce conscientious communities where there are collaborative, consultative, and cooperative voices and efforts. To make these efforts fruitful, it is critical to:

- Know the strengths and needs of children and families that drive services.
- Engage in comprehensive and cohesive services.
- Value the cultural backgrounds and norms of participants.
- Attach stable funding and resources to community-based efforts.
- Make very essential quality evaluation of services and programs.
- Build for the future by consistently seeking answers to perennial problems.

In some of today's communities, instead of progressive competitions that can advance and grow communities, there are competitions based on which communities can be more conservative and retrogressive. In some communities, there are unconscionable behaviors and actions that are taking place. They include the following:

- Book banning from schools and community libraries.
- Viewing diversity, equity, and inclusion programs as quota or irrelevant programs.
- Presuming ignorantly that racism is over.
- Infringing ruthlessly on rights of different citizens and people.
- Trampling upon basic women's right to choose, civil rights, voting rights, immigrant rights, and other rights with impunity.
- Digging in of community members in their anti-progressive beliefs and policies.

Though many of these behaviors might appear repugnant, people have rights to reveal their voices on important community, State, and national issues. One can now argue that all community voices may not be "good" voices for students and families that are traditionally disenfranchised, disadvantaged, disillusioned, demeaned because of their culture, language, gender, national origin, ability, and disability. This means that it is critical that we do what we can to:

- Remove community-based barriers that reinforce the traditional misidentification, misassessment, mislabeling/categorization, misplacement, and misinstruction of CLD students and families.
- Recalibrate ourselves to be conscientious people ready to develop conscientious communities where all stakeholders are visible, seen, heard, respected, and valued with promises to maximize their fullest potential.
- Create opportunities for people to come together in safe spaces to have fearless or hearty conversations and dialogs for the common good.
- Market what we are all about as a community of peoples—this means letting people know that we cannot tolerate divisive, close-minded, and bigoted behaviors.
- Celebrate our common mission and achievements and reward people who have devoted their time and energy to building bridges of human valuing, altruism, and caring.

Implications for Education

As indicated, communities cannot be divorced from schools and institutions that are located in them, and vice versa. Like all communities, CLD communities embrace community-oriented programs that enhance the well-being of their members (Ford, 1995; Obiakor et al., 2002). For example, Ford (1995) agreed that:

> African American community-sponsored programs are constructed and implemented through a variety of traditional and contemporary secular and nonsecular organizations. For many, Black church remains an important leadership institution within the African American community. It extends a host of outreach programs to support education at levels ranging from early childhood to adulthood. Individual churches may assume total responsibility or establish networks of collaboration with other churches, businesses, and community agencies, including the public school. (p. 249)

In consonance, other CLD communities such as Latinos, Asians, and Native Americans have similar intentions and strategies for revealing their needs and working with mainstream communities. Embedded in their outreach are their cultural and linguistic strengths that are functional in their interactions with educators, including general and special educators and vocational educators.

Typically, community voices advocate for community programs; and, they make programs to be cost effective to students, families, cities, and nation. For instance, using African American communities, Ford (1995) presented general, special, and vocational education programs that can benefit *ALL* learners, particularly those who come from CLD and vulnerable backgrounds. These programs include, but are not limited to:

- After-school tutoring.
- Latchkey programs.
- In-school tutoring by volunteers, mentors, and so on.
- Saturday programs—these may be independent or school-related assignments.
- Field trips of different dimensions.
- Workshops of different dimensions.
- Weekend retreats of different dimensions (e.g., how to pass standardized exams).
- Gender-specific programs—these may be Rites of Passage for males and females.
- Peer group activities.

- Short-term programs—these may be reading, art, poetry, and so on.
- Long-term programs—these may be programs offered by churches, service programs, work study programs, and so on.

It is important to realize that our communities have many people with special needs. Their voices deserve to be heard also! The situation becomes more intense when CLD and vulnerable families have children, youth, and adults with disabilities. The aforementioned programs can meet their unique needs and honor the fact that there are laws that protect their civil rights as human beings (Ford, 2002; Ford et al., 1995; Obiakor, 2007; Obiakor & Ford, 2002; Obiakor et al. 2019). For example, for those with physical and other health impairments, community houses and buildings must be accessible and their employability opportunities must be provided and protected. According to Ford et al. (2019), school-community partnerships are critical in enhancing innovative opportunities and resources and in maximizing the learning and life potentials of students, especially those who come from CLD and vulnerable backgrounds. Such partnerships are measurably successful when there are clarities in (a) intention, (b) collaboration, (c) communication, and (d) trust (see Ford et al., 2019).

Conclusion

This chapter has reiterated that community voices are important in education and society. Ignoring these voices is like driving a car without oil! This situation gets more critical in communities when we downplay, ignore, or silence voices of CLD and vulnerable families. Sadly, these families have children and youth with exceptionalities and at risk of being misidentified, misassessed, mislabeled/miscategorized, misplaced, and misinstructed. These family voices must be heard at their community and school levels (i.e., from pre-kindergarten to university levels). Generally, concrete efforts must be made to value community voices and help schools in program designs and implementations at on-campus and off-campus levels. This means that we must be creative in our community initiatives and make sure that educational accreditation agencies demonstrate integrity in making certain that community voices are culturally and linguistically responsive, functional, and goal-directed. If done right, community voices will prevent school dropouts, suspensions, expulsions, and jail/prison terms. Finally, we must make sure that there are collaborative and consultative energies to solve educational and societal problems of all communities, especially those of CLD and vulnerable populations. As Dooley and Toscano-Nixon (2002) conclusively pointed out:

> The values, mores, and beliefs held by community members are often imprinted into the school environment. The belief system held in a community is unique to that particular community. While the positive influences within a community can promote school achievement among students, the negative influences could interfere or hinder progress. When negative influences persist and very few community supports exist, all members, citizens, regardless of parental status must play a role in helping to define positive educational and social outcomes of children and youth within those communities. (pp. 101–102)

CHAPTER 10

WHY GOOD LEADERSHIP MATTERS IN MULTICULTURAL EDUCATION AND ADVANCEMENTS

ABSTRACT

Leadership can make or break an organization or institution. Even in family circles, leadership is critical in raising children and building families. So, good leadership is important in uplifting schools, colleges, universities, communities, nations, and world. The critical questions are, What makes a "good" leader? Does a good leader have to be affiliated to a race, culture, language, national origin, religion, to mention a few? These questions call for proper preparation of leaders who are ready to change or shift their paradigms and powers. This task is not (and will never be) easy in tumultuous environments where people who are "different" or come from culturally and linguistically diverse backgrounds (CLD) are intentionally or unintentionally disenfranchised, disadvantaged, disillusioned, and demeaned. This chapter explains why good leadership matters in multicultural education and advancements.

Keywords: Leadership; good leadership; valuing different "others," shifting paradigms and powers; developing people; building the future

Introduction

What defines leadership? Are all leaders good? Does one have to belong to a particular race, skin color, culture, linguistic group, religion, national origin, or gender to be a good leader? Does a good leader have to be of a particular political party? Does a good leader have to be handsome, beautiful, ugly, tall, fat, short, or physically fit? Does a good leader have to be God-made or man/woman-made? Can a good leader make a difference where bad leaders have failed? Can a bad leader be trained to be a good leader? These questions are multidimensional, thought-provoking, and even controversial. However, they can inspire more personal and systemic discourses and solutions that advance multiculturalism. Frequently, when decisions are made about leadership, we talk less about "**EFFECTIVENESS**" and talk more about "**FITNESS**." More than three decades ago, Steven R. Covey (1990), in his book, *The 7 Habits of Highly Effective People: Powerful Lessons in Personal Change* focused on characteristics of effective leaders who believe in change. According to Covey (1990), these habits are centered on:

- Being proactive.
- Beginning with the end in mind.
- Putting first things first.
- Thinking win-win.
- Seeking first to understand, then to be understood.
- Synergizing.
- Sharpening the saw.

The above habits involve paradigm and power shifts that are geared toward effective or good leadership. They are holistic and principled approaches aimed at solving personal, institutional, organizational, professional, community, national, and global problems. Following these approaches opens doors for measurability of attributes that enhance human valuing. However, in many quarters, leadership continues to focus of "fitness" which closes doors for measurability and accountability.

At this juncture, discussions about "fitness" deserve some attention. What "fitness" are we really referring to? From my perspective, systemic "fitness" does not truly lend itself to "innovation" or "change." "Fitness" to me, refers to sameness of race, culture, language, religion, national origin, or gender. And, "fitness" can also mean experience, agreeability, normativity, or other synchronizing qualities or variables. Clearly, "fitness" can be defined from the narrow perspective of what an organization wants or needs and which may also be antithetical to change and innovation. Put another way, "fitness" as a construct can be prejudicially assigned—this means that "fitness" can just be a label that is used to build up any person and make him/her more attractive than others in the competition. While we cannot realistically interrogate reasons for hiring a leader, we know, in the end, that a good leader is judged or determined on the bases of his/her positive productivity to an organization or a system. Nobody expects or should expect a leader to be perfect; however, a good leader usually creates harmonious and conscientious communities where everyone in the team feels at home and maximizes his/her fullest potential despite his/her race, culture, language, national origin, religion, or gender. This is the premise of this chapter.

What Good Leaders Do or Do Not Do

Leadership involves people and stability; and, it can be good, bad, and mediocre. The goal of any institution, organization, community, and nation is always to get and ensure good and stable leadership. When leadership is forced or imposed on people, which on its own is abnormal, abnormality and calamity take over, thereby creating rooms for more abnormalities and calamities. Leadership can advance harmony, peace, normalcy, and future. As humans, when we disturb normalcy, anarchy sets in and stays in. This is why every school, institution, organization, community, and nation seeks good leadership. Such leadership is usually awake, vigilant, and does not go to sleep; and further, it engineers quality, equanimity, and equity at all levels.

It is common knowledge that good leadership breeds excellence and equitability and divorces itself from mediocrity. In other words, good leadership understands that mediocrity breeds mediocrity! Based on my experiences, I have seen leaders who are incompetent and "ugly" in the ways they solve problems. In addition, I have seen organizations, institutions, and systems that consistently flirt with and hire mediocre leaders and still expect these individuals to make positive changes and miraculous innovations that sadly never occur. In reality, it is easy to see and measure good or bad leadership when "effectiveness" is at play; however, it is difficult when "fitness" is at play. Below are leadership cases that stem from my personal experiences:

Case of Dr. S

Dr. S was a White lady who served as Provost and Vice President for Academic Affairs of a university that is located in the Southern part of the United States. She used to give great speeches that melted our hearts. In these speeches, she frequently reminded us about the holocaust and pogrom. As an Igbo man from Nigeria who experienced pogrom during the Nigeria/Biafra war, I loved her speeches. However, she was very intimidating and tough on Black students, faculty, staff, and administrators. I was the only Black male in the College of Education—I saw hell and there was no one to talk to. One morning, I saw Dr. S at the parking lot where I packed my car. I greeted her, "Good morning, Dr. S;" and she responded, "What makes this morning a good morning?" I calmly responded, "It's a good morning to me." In my years in that university as an Assistant Professor, I worked very hard to improve my teaching even though students complained about my accent. As a researcher and scholar, I won the award of "Researcher of the Year" for two years in a roll in my department, College, and university. In my services, I was a well-known professional and citizen in the university, community, and nation. I was shocked that a human being like Dr. S can be that mean. I discovered that Dr. S hated culturally and linguistically diverse (CLD) faculty, staff, and administrator—she found it difficult to support their hiring, continuation, tenure, and promotion. Later, Dr. S did not support my continuation at that university even though most of my colleagues, my Chair, and Dean supported me. I was devastated and left for another university! I later heard that Dr. S left the university as a Provost to accept the Presidency of another university. Well, she lost her job in her first few months as President and joined the faculty of her new university. Ironically, I saw Dr. S as a faculty member when I was invited by her new university to interview for Deanship of the College of Education. Thinking back, Dr. S. was a bad, soulless, and culturally insensitive leader.

Case of Dr. N

Dr. N was a White female Chancellor of a university in the Midwest of the United States. I was one of the two senior scholars who she hired to work as Full Professors with tenure in the College of Education. She was cheerful, fashionable, and classy. She was a true scholar who continued to do her research and writing; and she held annual receptions for scholars in her home. Every two years, she had a powerful reception to honor all university book authors. She involved me in many activities—for example, I was the Faculty Recruitment Advisor of the Men's Basketball Team; and Dr. N appreciated that service. She invited me to talk with new recruits and took advantage of my strengths. She believed in putting the diversity, equity, and inclusion (DEI) into practice and she was loved on and off campus. She hired many people from CLD backgrounds and used the strengths that they brought to the table. It was no surprise that she left the university to another major Research 1 University to serve as President. A few years later, she went to New York to serve as the overall President of one of the two top systems in New York. Dr. N can be ranked as one of the best leaders that I worked with in higher education. Thinking back, Dr. N. was a good and culturally sensitive leader.

Case of Dr. A

Dr. A was an African American male Dean of a College of Education at a university located in the Midwest of the United States. As a senior faculty, I was one of the serious advocates of Dr. A during his interview for Deanship. During his interviews, Dr. A was not the sharpest kid on the block—his credentials were not up to par with the position that he had and wanted. Though his service was okay, his scholarship was disgraceful. In fact, when he was offered the job as Dean, his designated departmental faculty did not vote overwhelmingly for his tenure and promotion; and the university over-rode their decision! I was a top scholar in the College; and to gain trust amongst White colleagues, he eliminated all my supports to diminish my scholarly productivity. I was the only foreign-born Black male faculty; and he hated and detested me with a passion. While he compressed my salary and consistently gave others raises, he supported African American and White faculty members. He had support of university authorities—it was strange and difficult to live through this negative experience! Dr. A ranks as one of the worst Deans in my professional career—being an African American makes it more devastating. Thinking back, Dr. A. was a bad, xenophobic, and hateful leader.

Case of Dr. W

Dr. W was an African American Dean of a College of Education in a major Research 1 University. Before I came to this university, I was aware of his research and publications. In fact, he was involved in landmark works on the recruitment and retention of Black faculty. As a leader, he said what he meant and meant what he said. He was very dedicated to service and believed in DEI programs—he understood that Black voices are needed and what was at stake for the future of higher education. He rewarded hard work—faculty, staff, and administrators felt it. He provided resources that helped me to do my job and never played politics with productivity since he was also personally productive. Before long, he went forward to serve as Chief Executive Officer, Vice President, and very lately President at other organizations and institutions. I will rank him as one of the best Deans that I worked with. Thinking back, he was an effective leader.

Future Directions

It is clear that leadership matters at all levels; and, it is also clear that our leadership problems are real human problems. As I noted elsewhere,

> In many educational circles, we consistently see the victimization and silencing of "outside the box" culturally and linguistically diverse (CLD) voices. The *modus vivendi* has been to play games, work smart (not hard), join the herd mentality, be seen and not heard. In addition, we see visible circles of leadership failure and mediocrity that are devoid of measurable checks and balances on issues related to diversity. One is forced to ask, Who actually runs the show? (Obiakor, 2014, p. 123)

In our current leadership situations all over the world, it is still reasonable to ask, Who actually runs the show? We continue to do the same things, make the same mistakes, and expect different results. And, we consistently allow inept people to lead our organizations, institutions, and communities. Our leadership selection process is finally catching up with us. We know when leaders are racist, close-minded, xenophobic, and downright inimical; yet, we close our eyes, choose them to lead, and allow them to ruin people's lives because of one reason or another. As a people, do we not need leaders who may not be perfect but who equitably value fellow humans, understand human pains, and lead with a heart?

Looking at the aforementioned Cases, we see visibly good, bad, and mediocre leaders. In the Case of Dr. S, we have a totally soulless and brutal woman who showed blatant hateful behaviors to other people. She forgot that she was a leader in a very high position—she lacked multidimensionality in her duties as a leader. Though she understood wickedness and evil, she never went into the mind's eyes of others. I was the only Black male in the College of Education, and a very productive faculty for that matter; and, she still tried to destroy my career as many others have tried. In the Case of Dr. N, we see a leader who understood the very nature of leadership—she was able to elevate the university's presence locally, nationally, and internationally. Though she was not perfect, she led with a heart. In the Case of Dr. A, we have a man who is lost in quandary. People like him help in devaluing the DEI project—he represents diversity, but not a good one. In short, he represented a "BAD DIVERSITY." His incompetence was clear and he wallowed in mediocrity and ineptness most of the time. Sadly, based on my experiences, the White racist system seems to hire and promote inept people like Dr. A. And, in the Case of Dr. W, we see a leader who knew what was at stake. He was a man who (a) performed his job with a heart; (b) valued the uniqueness of human beings; and (c) helped his students, faculty, staff, and administrators to maximize their potential.

There is no doubt that we need good and effective leaders who are willing to shift their paradigms and powers to be innovative and change-oriented (Obiakor et al., 2017). According to Obiakor et al. (2017), effective leadership must:

- Be adaptive (i.e., makes necessary adjustments).
- Act on a setting (i.e., observes contexts to solve problems).
- Empower (i.e., inspires confidence).
- Act on people's feelings (i.e., finds ways to understand instincts).
- Create contributions (i.e., understands strengths that people bring to the table).
- Be about problem-solving (i.e., works on solutions).
- Foster creativity (i.e., enables people to use their imaginations).

These leadership skills might be slated for leaders who work with special needs children and youth; however, they can be used by all leaders who are interested in making a positive difference in the lives of different "others" at all educational levels (i.e., pre-kindergarten to university levels). And, to make a positive difference, such leaders must be culturally sensitive and responsive and be willing to shift their paradigms and powers as needed (McCray & Beachum, 2014; McCray et al., 2021; Obiakor et al., 2017).

In Chris Donnelly's (2024) *Leadership Green Flags*, he reiterated the need for great and creative leaders who can:

- *Ask for your feedback on the company's culture*—they care about maintaining and sustaining the company's tradition and culture.
- *Take an interest in your life outside of work*—they want to know you as a person, not a number.
- *Never schedule meetings over lunch*—they respect the fact that lunch is your time to recharge and fuel up.
- *Ask for your ideas*—they want everyone to be involved in decisions.
- *Follow up or act on the feedback that you give*—they act and implement with speed.
- *Give every room they walk into a burst of energy*—they make their presence to be inspiring.
- *Get stuck in with the day-to-day when needed*—they set the example, they won't just command.
- *Set boundaries and respect yours in return*—they understand the importance of boundaries.
- *Praise in public and discipline in private*—they respect you and your reputation.
- *Be transparent about their plans*—they want everyone to be aligned.
- *Share the rewards of the business' success*—they never give it all to themselves.
- *Give credit where it is due*—they praise consistently for hard work.

Conclusion

This chapter reiterates the fact that good leadership matters; and, we must be clear about that. In every environment and at every level, it is impossible to divorce leadership from multicultural education and interactions. This means that we need innovative and transformative leaders who will inspire individuals to think their ways into a system of living instead of living their ways into a pattern of thinking. Such transformative leaders must use their voices and skills to recruit, retain, and promote diverse voices in their institutions and organizations. Finally, to achieve futuristic goals, we need innovative leaders who can:

- Encourage heterogeneity in policies as they relate to race, culture, language, national origin, socio-economics, religion, gender, talent, and disability.

- Initiate "hearty" and fearless conversations and safe spaces that synchronize with usually well-written institutionalized statements of vision, mission, goals, objectives, and values.
- Motivate invisible voices to be more visible and active for the common good.
- Think, see, hear, and talk in non-offensive, non-hateful, and non-prejudicial ways.
- Practice what they say and say what they practice to avoid confusing inconsistencies that disrupt organizational flow and harmony.

CHAPTER 11

WHY THE COMPREHENSIVE SUPPORT MODEL MATTERS IN MULTICULTURAL EDUCATION AND INTERACTIONS

ABSTRACT

The comprehensive support model (CSM) is a model that values the collective energies of students, families, schools, communities, and government agencies in solving critical educational and societal problems. The CSM takes advantage of collaborative, consultative, and cooperative pillars that fortify human interactions and buttress diversity, equity, inclusion, quality, harmony, peace, growth, and success. And, to a large measure, the CSM prevents and reduces (a) prejudicial expectations and jaundiced views; (b) inhumane hateful interactions; (c) traditional misidentification, misassessment, mislabeling/miscategoriation, misplacement, and miseducation; and (d) individual and societal disenfranchisements, disadvantages, and disillusionments. Clearly, not hearing or valuing ALL voices is a danger to the well-being of humanity. This chapter expands why the CSM matters in multicultural education and interactions.

Keywords: The CSM; collaboration and consultation; building harmony; reducing prejudice and hate; increasing voices and productivity; solidifying multiculturalism

Introduction

Very often, we get excited about team-work in educational sectors and workplaces. We also get excited when institutions, organizations, and communities practice team-work. However, time and time again, the kind of team-work that we see is the one that excludes and victimizes different groups of people for one reason or the other. For example, in schools and communities, team works exclude students and families who are atypical or who come from culturally and linguistically diverse (CLD) and vulnerable backgrounds (Obiakor, 2001, 2008; Obiakor et al., 2002). A classroom or school program usually involves different students, families, and educational professionals. These individuals are supposed to work together to achieve their targeted goals. The questions are, What happens when they do not work or refuse to work together? What happens when one of the groups refuses to work with others (e.g., families versus teachers)? What happens when group members are racist, xenophobic, prejudicial, close-minded, to mention a few? These are scenarios that can play themselves out in collaborative, consultative, and cooperative contexts and engagements.

As indicated, team-work is one of the engines of educational programming. The problem is that sometimes school personnel do not practice what they preach—they disrespect and look down on parents, especially when they come from CLD and vulnerable backgrounds. Though these unconscionable behaviors consistently take place, there are usually zero consequences for engaging in them. Consider the following scenario:

The Case of the Faculty Lounge

As a college professor, I frequently visited schools for research, service, and practicum obligations and activities. During such visits, I hear a lot, see a lot, ask a lot, and wonder a lot! During one of my visits, I was in one school's faculty lounge where I saw and heard teachers and leaders make evil and negative comments about an African American student and his family to their colleagues. Sadly, their colleagues were in immediate agreement and joined them in talking bad and negative about that student and family who they never knew or met before. I was shocked that nobody called them out for their unprofessional and hateful behaviors. Rather, they abetted such unprofessionalism, negativism, prejudice, and hate towards their clients. Apparently, they were enjoying a fake sense of collegial community and a real sense of cultural and racist antagonism.

Sadly, these are the kinds of unprofessional behaviors that go down in many schools' faculty lounges. These behaviors make it very difficult to understand, trust, and rely on a teacher or related professional, even if he/she acts puritanically like a professional saint. Despite problems of this nature, educators are professionally and legally obligated to do their jobs as well-trained and knowledgeable people who meet the multi-dimensional needs of students and families on and off school campuses.

As a tradition, educational professionals pride themselves on collaboratively working together to maximize the fullest potential of students. The reasons are simple—students cannot teach themselves and teachers cannot be optimally successful when they try to do everything on their own. This means that educational professionals need the CSM to enhance measurable collaborative, consultative, and cooperative energies from their students, other school personnel, families, community members, and government agencies (see Obiakor, 2001, 2008; Obiakor et al., 2002). In addition, these professionals must take advantage of the collective strengths and supports that come from all stakeholders. Elsewhere, I suggested that we take advantage of these collaborative supports to create positive results that can only be achieved through the CSM (Obiakor, 2001, 2008; Obiakor et al., 2002). The CSM is a mutually inclusive and exclusive model that connects strong individual entities to work together for the common good. Further, the CSM inspires these entities to remain open and permit other entities to come in to boost innovation and change. Amazingly, the CSM upholds and nurtures the African principle of "IT TAKES A VILLAGE TO RAISE A CHILD."

I acknowledge that the CSM is not a panacea for solving all the problems that confront education today and in the future. However, the CSM will assist *ALL* targeted and responsible stakeholders to:

- Diagnostically identify students' school, family, and societal problems very early.
- Formatively assess the consistent disenfranchisements, disadvantages, and disillusionments that students face at all educational and community levels.
- Summatively prescribe solutions to students' endemic problems at all levels.
- Futuristically create pathways for paradigm and power shifts at all students' educational and societal levels.

This chapter aims at appreciating and valuing the CSM as a team work approach to problem-solving in educational processes from pre-kindergarten to university levels. Embedded in this discussion are the impacts of the CSM on multicultural education and interactions.

Contextualizing the CSM

As indicated, the CSM sets the stage for collaborative ventures at all educational and societal levels. It values *ALL* voices of stakeholders and recognizes their roles in the critical processes of seeing, hearing, speaking, feeling, and doing. But, it also gets them involved in hard non-fluffy issues of civil rights, laws, curricula, materials/equipment, methods, and processes. All of these make the whole processes and routes of education to be fully analyzed, synthesized, and evaluated. In other words, the CSM motivates stakeholders to:

- Put all hands on deck.
- Create opportunities for CLD and vulnerable persons to be a part of a productive team.
- Make sure that atypical persons and voices are participating in discourses that concern them.
- Help to personally and systemically shift paradigm and powers at all educational levels.
- Make sure that solid plans are made to buttress change and advance the future.
- Recapture the powerful processes of diagnostic, formative, and summative evaluations in education at all levels.

Based on the collective participation and performance of the CSM, some important questions deserve to be asked in educational collaborative ventures. Following are these questions:

- Why are we here? Do we all have the interest convergence to do our jobs correctly?
- What is our purpose? Do we have the unity-of-purpose?
- What is our vision? What is our mission?
- What are our goals? What are our objectives?
- What are our rules of engagement? Are we equal partners?
- What is our memorandum of understanding?
- Are we hearing all voices or some voices?
- Are we respecting all voices or some voices?
- Are we seeing everyone or some of us?
- Are we documenting all our thoughts or some of our thoughts?
- Are we making sure that no voice is silenced?
- Are we making sure that no one is invisible?
- Are we all in a safe space?
- Are we all culturally and linguistically sensitive?
- Are we relating to all values or some of the values brought to the table?
- Are we communicating as equal partners who cherish the common good?

- Are our dispositions heart-warming or inimical in our collaborative lens?
- What are CLD students thinking, saying, and doing?
- What are CLD families thinking, saying, and doing?
- What are the school personnel thinking, saying, and doing?
- What are CLD community members thinking, saying, and doing?
- What are government agencies thinking, saying, and doing?
- What are our points of agreements and our points of disagreements?
- What actions will follow our agreements?
- What happens if decisions and actions are not yielding fruitful dividends?
- How and when should our successes be celebrated?
- After this, what else? How do we solidify successes and move forward?

Looking at the above questions, one can conclusively see how collaborative engagements can lead to personal and community uplifts. These questions will expose the CSM's ability to:

- Interrogate the existing status quo.
- Disrupt the traditional equilibrium.
- Stimulate change.
- Welcome discourses that challenge traditions.
- Shift paradigms and powers.
- Create environments that are culturally and linguistically welcoming and relatable to all.
- Advance human respect and valuing of participants and stakeholders.
- Maximize positive collaborative engagements and productivities.

The Functionality of the CSM in Education

It is no secret that educators and related practitioners enjoy talking about *change* even though they do not or rarely engage in change themselves. In the same dimension, they talk about team-work and frequently resist team-work, especially when it involves people of other races, cultures, languages, values, religions, genders, and so on. The fact remains that team-work actually works if and when we take advantage of the CSM to maximize the collaborative spirits, strengths, and energies of *students, families, schools, communities, and government agencies* (see Obiakor, 2001; Obiakor et al., 2002). Not valuing the functionality of the CSM is educationally retrogressive and counterproductive; and silencing any voice in the CSM, as atypical as it might seem, is inimical and non-futuristic.

More so, the functionality of the CSM sheds light on the functionality of collaborative human spirits and endeavors to solve challenging human problems. From an African-centered perspective, it is believed, "when you go to war alone, you can either win alone or you lose alone." This may be shocking to many in the Western world (e.g., the United States) where people arrogantly assume that "they are self-made people." Though I understand the contextual value of their statement, I also understand the contextual error or danger of their statement. The reality is that we all rely somehow on others depending on the situation or circumstance.

Student's Visibility

In all situations, we need collective energy. For example, we all believe our children and youth are our prime possessions. Spiritually, we view them as gifts from God—this is especially true for Christians. But, in our societies today, we treat our children and youth as disposable commodities. This thinking seems to generate more questions than answers, as seen below:

- How can any right thinking human being abuse, molest, sell, and enslave our kids?
- Why do leaders during wars bomb places where children reside?
- Why do we continue to see old men marry people younger than their grandchildren in the name of religion or culture?
- Why do parents abandon their children in the name of poverty?
- Why do we even see politicians politicize child welfare or food stamp programs?
- Why do governments not seriously invest in programs that could salvage the plights of our children?
- Why do we not like to hear our children's voices (i.e., what children think) as we work with them?

Based on the above questions, one can see that we have been short-selling our children and that our cups have been half-full when it comes to children's programs. The CSM makes children and students its first entity because our educational programs revolve around them (Obiakor, 2001, 2008; Obiakor et al., 2002). It makes students equal partners in their educational processes. The fact remains that we cannot work with children when we silence their voices and make them invisible in any educational encounter. And, for students with special needs or those who come from CLD backgrounds, we should involve them (if they want to) in their individualized education program (IEP) discussions. We must get out of the habit of misidentifying, misassessing, mislabeling/miscategorizing, misplacing, and misinstructing students just because they have special needs or come from CLD, at-risk, and vulnerable backgrounds. Based on CSM, students' voices are needed and must be cherished—they are our customers and clients (Obiakor, 2001, 2008; Obiakor et al., 2002).

Family's Visibility

As indicated, children come from families to schools. So, ignoring families makes no educational or logical sense. When families are not given adequate supports in raising their children, we make them to be disenfranchised, disadvantaged, and disillusioned. Parents love and know their children—they know what is reinforcing or discouraging to them; and most of them do whatever it takes to raise them. Why then do teachers and related professionals undervalue and un-value them, silence their voices, and use derogatory labels to describe them in *faculty lounges?* Even when they are economically "poor," it does not necessarily mean that they are "poor" mentally, socially, and emotionally; and when they are "rich," it does not really mean that they are "rich" mentally, socially, and emotionally. Similarly, we cannot afford to insult parents' homes and neighborhoods since we now know that crimes and abominations happen in all neighborhoods. Based on the CSM, families are equal partners in educational processes; and we must keep it that way (Obiakor, 2001, 2008; Obiakor et al., 2002).

School's Visibility

The CSM respects and values teachers and school personnel (see Obiakor, 2001, 2008; Obiakor et al., 2002). Many school professionals do excellent jobs; and some do not! In addition, some of them are lost in quandary. Nonetheless, their importance is known and valued world-wide because of what they do and how they do what they do. Many of them are caring and well prepared by educator preparation programs; however, many of them are ill-prepared, unprepared, disastrous, dangerous, and do not mind tarnishing the reputation of their wonderful profession. For example, a teacher once told me, "I DO NOT LOVE CHILDREN." How can that be? How can a teacher not love the main reason for his/her job? How can a teacher be racist, xenophobic, inhumane, hateful, and socio-emotionally not ready and still be a teacher to any human being? Today, there are teachers and educational professionals who carry such negative baggage and still find themselves in schools, colleges, and universities.

Most human beings are caring and culturally responsive. However, some of them have continued to maintain the Eurocentric myth on "goodness" and "brilliance," that is, that making and maintaining good grades and grade point averages depict a good student, person, or teacher. Using this Eurocentric perspective to recruit, retain, reward, and promote CLD students, faculty, staff, administrators, and leaders goes against diversity, equity, and inclusion policies and moves us backwards. All educational personnel must have the needed culturally responsive qualities to be functionally successful from pre-kindergarten to university levels. These qualities must include:

- Caring dispositions.
- Excellent academic acumen.
- Inviting or welcoming personality.
- Common sense attributes.
- Soulful and hearty non-prejudicial actions.
- Collaborative and consultative spirits.

Not respecting these principles destroys education and human dignity which all educational institutions and organizations are supposed to protect and advance (see Obiakor, 2001, 2008, 2018, 2020, 2021, 2023a, 2023b; Obiakor et al., 2002). This means that we need educational professionals who believe in the integrity and sanctity of their profession.

Community's Visibility

Just as students, families, and school personnel should be treated with dignity, communities should also be treated with decency. In the CSM, communities are equal partners who should not be ignored, downplayed, or labeled (Obiakor, 2001, 2008, 2018, 2020, 2021, 2023b; Obiakor et al., 2002). Sadly, many of our communities, especially those with predominantly CLD children, youth, and families are consistently undervalued and insulted. As noted, evil and wicked acts take place in almost all communities. Why then should we disrespect some and honor others? In our communities, many of our worthy institutions and organizations are housed and functional. While our communities can be urban, suburban, or rural, they consistently house our schools, colleges/universities, churches, mosques, synagogues, hospitals, work places, recreational facilities, police stations, jails/prisons, shopping malls, grocery stores, restaurants, and hotels, to mention a few. All of these are nurtured and protected because they provide resources that also help to nurture and protect our lives. In special education, communities play tremendous roles (e.g., providing service learning and vocational education and providing employment opportunities to people with exceptionalities). Clearly, it is no surprise that (a) institutions and organizations have community representatives or liaisons, (b) community members serve as board members in institutions/organizations, and (c) educational accrediting agencies want to hear community voices to ascertain if institutions and organizations have value-added benefits to communities. In the end, we will be well-served if and when we understand that people make up communities and communities make up people.

Government's Visibility

The government is an important pillar in the CSM (Obiakor et al., 2002). Ignoring government agencies is like ignoring the father, mother, or caretaker of the house. State and federal governments usually have agencies that play critical roles on students, schools, families, and communities. Government agencies try to make sure that legal and civil rights of *ALL* people are protected; and they fund programs to make sure that monies are available for much needed programs. Additionally, they make sure that systemic rules and regulations are not abused. By doing this, they expand opportunities to CLD persons who are disenfranchised, disadvantaged, and disillusioned. At state levels, educational programs are accredited with certain provisions and designs. With the government's presence, programs are systemically managed and infused to manage freedom, rights, and directions. Serious problems come to play when the government's accrediting agencies fail to hold people, institutions, and organizations accountable. There must be penalties for entities that violate critical responsibilities of civil and systemic rights.

Multicultural Implications of the CSM

It is clear that the CSM is intertwined with collaboration, consultation, and cooperation and their connectivity to students, families, schools, communities, and government agencies. Embedded in these powerful connections are people of diverse racial, cultural, linguistic, and religious values, to mention a few (Obiakor, 2001, 2008; Obiakor et al., 2002). Based on the CSM, people have equal rights and obligations to do what is right and have their voices heard at the same time. Ignoring any of the stakeholders will cause harm to the overall systemic flow of the CSM.

As noted, students from CLD and vulnerable backgrounds have continued to experience negative encounters from pre-kindergarten to university levels. As a result, allowing them to share their experiences is the correct move. It is impossible to solve their problems without hearing from them and involving them in the processes. Usually, their vulnerable families also fall into the same racist trap. It is morally wrong to silence the voices of these families who already feel disenfranchised and demeaned. The CSM gives ample opportunities to CLD and vulnerable families to share their ideas on how to deal with eventual school problems.

It is important to reiterate that educational personnel are a part of the CSM—they can make and unmake. They are supposed to treat CLD students and families with care and humanity. And, their job is not to discriminate, underrate, disparage, and ignore CLD and vulnerable students who are under their watch. To a large measure, these students are supposed to be inspired to maximize their fullest potential. As a consequence, school personnel must be thoroughly prepared by educator preparation programs to be culturally sensitive and responsive at all times and at all educational levels. In fact, school districts and colleges/universities should recruit, tenure, and promote CLD faculty, staff, administrators, and leaders who can serve as good role models and examples for CLD students and their families.

As indicated, all communities are critical elements of the CSM. For CLD communities, the goal must be treat them as equal partners who have a lot to share. Communities around CLD persons must provide interactional facilities like play grounds for at-risk children and youth. They can recruit and employ workers and assistants who also come from CLD backgrounds. CLD communities must be heard and involved in the educational processes in nondiscriminatory ways. In the CSM, government agencies are supposed to uphold the civil and legal rights of everyone and provide funding opportunities for CLD and vulnerable populations. They must be equitable in delivering their services and make sure that all voices are seen, heard, and allowed to speak.

Conclusion

This chapter presents the CSM as a collaborative, consultative, and cooperative entity that brings students, families, schools, communities, and government agencies together to value each other and work for the common and/or collective good. It is a philosophical and practical model that goes beyond the rhetoric of what is and what is not. People talk about multiculturalism; however, the CSM puts it into practical perspectives. CLD students are learners who have unique voices that are frequently silenced. We need to know what they think and how we can help to maximize their fullest potential. These students and their families cannot do this alone. Instead of devaluing CLD families in *faculty lounges*, proactive efforts must be made to hear their voices. They can be great informants to us, if we use them correctly and respectfully. This means that our school personnel from pre-kindergarten to university levels must be well trained and prepared to be responsible entities in culturally and linguistically sensitive manners. Our communities must work hand-in-glove with students, families, school personnel, and government agencies at all levels to initiate creative programs that will reduce hate and advance harmony. And, our government agencies cannot afford to be silent actors who also believe in silencing other voices. These agencies must value and espouse democratic nondiscriminatory ideals at all governmental levels. Finally, all government agencies must make sure that all people are visible, all voices are heard, all rights are respected, and all properties are protected in responsible ways.

CHAPTER 12

WHY GLOBAL EDUCATION MATTERS IN MULTICULTURAL EDUCATION AND INTERACTIONS

ABSTRACT

We live in a global world; and what happens in one region of the world affects other regions, in one form or another. Examples include (a) diseases such as coronavirus, acquired immunodeficiency syndrome, and Ebola; and (b) conflicts and wars such as Mid-East conflicts/wars, Ukraine-Russia war, and terrorist attacks. While the independence of countries reflects socio-economic and political emancipation and freedom, the interdependence of countries is sometimes doubted by megalomaniac citizens or leaders with colonial, supremacist, and discriminatory viewpoints. This very narrow perspective of the world is disgraceful, sad, and retrogressive; yet, it is popular in many quarters of the world. Ironically, most institutions and organizations in the world (e.g., in education, healthcare, and business) pride themselves on having global perspectives as reflected in their core vision and mission statements. Oftentimes, the rhetoric overshadows the practice! This chapter reiterates why it is imperative that educational institutions from pre-kindergarten to university levels focus on proactive ways to initiate and stabilize global education and improve multiculturalism in the world.

Keywords: Global education and perspective; independence and freedom; interdependence and cooperation; world peace and harmony; sustainability; multiculturalism

Introduction

Today, countries all over the world celebrate their independence and freedom. While they continue to advance their sustainability, they all exist in an interdependent global society. We do understand that no person can be an island and that no nation can exist in isolation. Events taking place in distant countries have continued to impact our daily lives. New global sectors of social, economic, political, and educational developments are now having measurable effects on how we educate and train learners for work and life. In America and the world over, we are seeing some serious attention to current global shifts in paradigm and powers that are influencing daily activities and moves. As a consequence, we are all under pressure to recalibrate, reorganize, rethink, readjust, remodify, and reform our strategies to survive, excel, and beat our competitions (Obiakor, 2018, 2020, 2021, 2023a, 2023b).

It is evident that America and the rest of the world are increasingly diverse. However, it also appears that our educators and related professionals have failed to take full advantage of the diversities that will harmonize and unite our larger world. In perspective, we seem to be unaware that recent technological advancements and demographic and cultural forces can assist us in dramatically changing higher education landscapes around the world. Presently, we have not faced the reality that technology allows learners to (a) see the same advertisements, (b) enjoy the same entertainments, and (c) listen to the same news reports regardless of locations. To this effect, some relevant questions come to mind. They include:

- Why should our learners and professionals not understand how life in their cultural communities and nations influence other communities and nations?
- Why should our citizens not understand that international events and situations have cogent influences on their daily lives?
- Why should our world not take advantage of the laudable advances that have brought previously excluded voices into the conversations about educational access, achievement, and relevance?
- Why should our world not be worried about the wrongful use of technology to intensify xenophobia, racism, religious dogmatism, and homophobia?
- Why should our citizens not take advantage of the benefits of global and multicultural education and interactions to make our world a better place?

The above questions reveal the need to do something about individual and collective understanding and interactions. We can longer sweep our problems under the rug (see Obiakor, 2018, 2020, 2021, 2023b). We truly need functional and quantifiable answers that will move our world forward and yield practical human changes that have well-intentioned global, multicultural, and educational perspectives. This is the focus of this chapter.

The Crux of the Matter

We can no longer arrogantly pretend that we do not need different "others" and the world. The fact remains that if we do not need the people of the world, we should not be shocked to know that they may not in good faith need us. Having this knowledge is critical in helping us to (a) recharge our batteries of knowledge, (b) refocus our attention on the benefits of global education and multicultural interactions, (c) reemphasize and recalibrate our thinking about the world, and (d) reenergize our strengths to reach new levels (see Obiakor, 2018, 2020, 2021, 2023b). The questions then are, Do our schools and institutions understand the benefits of connecting ourselves to the world beyond our narrow confines? Do our educator preparation programs understand our stand in the world and our obligations to the world? It is important to note that traditional teacher educators have frequently endorsed global and multicultural education and interactions based on their website statements about mission, vision, values, priorities, goals, and objectives to reaffirm their authentic existence. However, these programs have been half-hearted in pragmatically tackling these issues. As it stands, with all the push-backs about diversity, equity, and inclusion (DEI), these programs are now faced with an urgent responsibility to transform curriculum and pedagogy to better prepare teachers and related professionals to operate in an increasingly global and interdependent world. It is time that these educational programs embraced change and redefined their roles in the emerging and competitive global society.

Yes, we are all affected by socio-political and economic changes around the world; however, it is unclear if we truly know what this entails. For example, we have tensions all over the world and global problems of poverty, environmental pollution, natural disaster, and wars have had far-reaching consequences on global understanding and world peace. Since we live in a global village, it is important that we develop a consciousness of how what is happening in one part of the globe influences other parts of the globe. While this awareness involves proactively developing economic, political, and social interrelationships and connections that are critical to our survival as human beings, it also exposes the far-reaching implications of this connectivity to multicultural education throughout the world. To a large measure, it has become seriously imperative to take advantage of our global and multicultural interactions in our diverse world to make it richer, safer, more relatable, more peaceful, and more advanced.

Global Contexts of Education

As indicated, understanding global relationships goes beyond local, regional, and national boundaries. This understanding is not only crucial in the United States, it is also crucial in other parts of the world. We know that recent demographic changes in America's school population call for measurable changes in educational theory, curriculum, and teaching strategies. And, new immigrants require paradigm shifts in teaching and learning, thereby creating new realities and relationships that engender new conditions of interdependency (Gutek, 2006). Based on these new realities and demands, how do we educate learners to function in an interdependent multicultural world?

To understand the global contexts on education, we must understand what cultural and human valuing entails. In addition, we must be in tune with the meaning of multicultural education as a progressive approach for transforming education that holistically critiques and addresses current shortcomings, failings, and discriminatory practices in the larger society. Gorski (2001) explained that multicultural education is grounded in the ideals of social justice and educational equity and facilitates educational experiences in which all students reach their full potential as learners. To a larger extent, global education involves learning about those problems and issues that go across national boundaries, and about the interconnectedness of ecological, cultural, economic, political, and technological systems. Also, global education involves perspective taking (i.e., seeing things through the eyes and minds of others) and elucidates the reality that individuals and groups may view life differently and still have common needs and wants (Tye, 1991).

Clearly, to buttress global and multicultural education and interactions, the role and impact of multimedia technology on classroom and outside experiences must be felt. Multimedia technology brings the world closer and closer to the learner and helps educators and service providers to create situations that stimulate interests, generate questions, find answers, and motivate investigations. Most importantly, it fosters freer communications between peoples, including those from culturally and linguistically diverse (CLD) backgrounds (Fabris, 1992). For instance, wireless devices, handheld computers, e-books, voice-activated devices, portable storages, microprocessors, and virtual environments have continued to allow learners to see the same advertisements, enjoy the same entertainments, and listen to the same news reports. Additionally, instructional technologies have continued to promote active involvement of students in the learning process and in assisting them to access and organize information (Jonassen et al., 2003; Maccini et al., 2002). These technologies are powerful tools for investigation, problem-solving, and creative expression; and, they are also tools that have created highly sophisticated learning environments in which knowledge is constructed, while being sensitive to each learner's needs in an economically acceptable fashion. To this end, I propose *four* critical imperatives, namely:

- Instituting global and multicultural education to become the heart of educational programs from pre-kindergarten to university levels around the world.
- Motivating educational leaders and professionals to develop visionary programs that inter-marry with knowledge, comprehension, application, analysis, synthesis, and evaluation.
- Calling for a future where multicultural literacy is developed and required for school personnel to understand the role of technology in working with all learners, including those from vulnerable and at-risk backgrounds.
- Making sure that learners possess the knowledge and skills on when and how to strategically apply technology that will in turn help them to solve instructional problems with greater success and build safer multicultural spaces.

As it stands, people are no longer spending their lives in one nation-state. Globalization trends and developments are significantly influencing citizens throughout the world and challenging national borders. The number of nations in the world is increasing rather than decreasing; and this increase continues to impact how teachers prepare learners to function in the global community (Banks, 1998; Obiakor, 2008; Obiakor et al., 2010). A significant challenge facing educators is how to best respect and acknowledge community cultures and learners' knowledge while at the same time helping them to construct a democratic public community with an overarching set of values to which all learners will have a commitment. This implies that educators and service providers must help learners to:

- Understand their cultural knowledge.
- Learn the benefits or consequences of embracing this cultural knowledge.
- Understand how cultural knowledge relates to mainstream academic knowledge of the world.
- Survive and participate effectively in their cultural communities, other cultural communities, the mainstream culture, and in the global community.

Moving Forward

Our overall global goal must be to build peace and harmony by educating learners to be effective citizens in their cultural communities, nation-states, and world community. It is important to revise the curriculum in substantial ways so that it reflects the complex national identities that are emerging in nation-states throughout the world. This is a difficult but essential task since it involves creating a positive global community (Banks, 1998; Obiakor, 2008). People of all ages, at all places, and in all different environments are learning all the time; many are updating their knowledge and skills in whatever they are doing to buttress global valuing. At the same time, objectives of education seem to be more complicated—it is not sufficient anymore to teach a certain body of knowledge and skills. On the one hand, learners are expected to acquire higher levels of cognitive skills (e.g., problem solving, creativity, collaborative learning, synthesis, and above all the skill of how to apply acquired knowledge to new situations). On the other hand, they are required to learn new information and communication technologies that facilitate new ways of learning in fast changing technology-based societies and economies.

Moving forward, we must collectively develop and expand education that is aimed at preparing professionals and learners to function within and across national borders. Because of the effects of globalization on citizens and nations throughout the world, educators and service providers must conceptualize ways to educate learners to function in a world that is being transformed by technology (Martin & Widgren, 2002; Sassen, 1998). From my perspective, global and multicultural education buttressed by technology can help learners from diverse cultural, racial, language, and religious groups to critically understand and examine their cultural identifications and attachments (Obiakor, 2008; Obiakor et al., 2010). In addition, such an education should give learners the option to maintain their cultural attachments and identifications as well as the option to endorse other cultures and identities. A genuine option should require that the school curriculum be revised so that it reflects the cultures of the diverse groups that make up the society. The emphasis must be on the education that helps students to acquire attitudes, knowledge, and skill-sets needed to function in cultural communities other than their own, within the national culture and community, as well as within the global community. To a large measure, educators and service providers must inspire students to (a) develop understandings of the interdependence among nations, (b) clarify attitudes toward nations and peoples, and (c) identify with the commonalities and differences of the world community as a whole.

Conclusion

It is clear that we live in a global village where multicultural knowledge and technological advancements are critical. Since students' needs are diverse, information and communication technologies can provide valuable contributions. As indicated, these technologies are becoming more flexible, unconstrained by time and place, and can be used on demand to provide just-in-time training. To a large measure, they offer synchronous and asynchronous learning opportunities to all (Villanuena, 1999). One of the most interesting yet challenging tasks for educators worldwide is how to conceptualize and develop guidelines and benchmarks that will help develop education courses and programs suitable for a globalized approach to learning. These courses and programs will enable learners to acquire the values and skill-sets needed to become effective citizens within a global context.

Finally, as problem-solvers and change agents in education, we owe it to the world to bring people together through education. We must zero in on global and multicultural education that helps all stakeholders to develop reflective global attachments that will yield solution-based foci on the world's difficult problems such as poverty, diseases, global warming, racism, conflicts, and wars. If we can collaboratively, consultatively, and cooperatively solve these problems, we would have done our part in making the world a better place to live.

CHAPTER 13

WHY ADVANCING MULTICULTURAL SKILLS MATTERS IN LIFE JOURNEYS

ABSTRACT

Human-beings are different, unique, and atypical; and they are different intra-individually and inter-individually. In addition, these differences are encapsulated in life journeys and reflected in skin color, race, national origin, gender, religion, culture, and language, to mention a few. This is why any kind of generalization, presumption, discrimination, prejudice, or bigotry against anyone can lead to intentional or unintentional misidentification, misassessment, mislabeling/miscategorization, misplacement, and miseducation. It then behooves general and special education practitioners and professionals to understand that each person has his/her personal idiosyncrasies and life journeys. In other words, these professionals must develop the multicultural skill-sets to work with ALL people and sectors, including culturally and linguistically diverse (CLD) and vulnerable students, parents, professional colleagues, communities, institutions, and organizations in the United States and other parts of the world. This chapter synthesizes why advancing multicultural skills matters in life journeys.

Keywords: Human-beings; life journeys; difference and uniqueness; prejudicial assumption; professional preparation; advancing multicultural skills and journeys

Introduction

In whatever we decide to do or become in life, we must be knowledgeable about it and do it right to be successful. And, since human beings are different, their individual success rates in their chosen journeys are destined to be different (Minton & Schneider, 1980). However, with learned skill-sets, individual efforts, and paradigm shifts, success rates and life circumstances of individuals can measurably and positively change. This means that there are important multicultural and socio-cultural tools that we need to meander through life's stages (Baron & Byrne, 1994; Obiakor, 2021). The question then is, Why is it critical to acquire multicultural tools in life despite who we think we are and where our directions are going? This chapter summarizes why we need well-intentioned multicultural skills that can assist us in successfully navigating through different mazes in our educational, employment, and life journeys.

Inside Our Life Journeys

Our life journeys begin with our births into this world; and, we are born into homes and families of different backgrounds. These family spaces function with different operational modes. In our unique home/family backgrounds, there are loaded differences in culture, religion, skin color, ethnic identity, socio-economics, language, political orientation, and national origin, to mention a few (Obiakor, 2021). Undermining these differences can cause socio-emotional scars of far-reaching proportions. In our cultural home/family enclave, nature and nurture converge and interplay with each other. In other words, in our interwoven journeys, our unique natural attributes begin to interact steadily with our environmental attributes. And, all these attributes are loaded with socio-cultural variables that are integral to human interaction, existence, and sustainability (Byron & Byrne, 1994).

Moving forward in life, the environment begins to seriously play dominant roles while the home/family continues to play its traditional role. In this environment, human beings go through different socio-cultural stages and steps. These critical stages present educational journeys for human survival and success. For example, in kindergarten, there are unique learning experiences that present necessary growths and challenges. In elementary schools, the experiences are also unique and challenging. In middle schools, there are teenage growth changes that are challenging; and, high schools create positive and negative challenges that are needed to boost man/woman hood. After graduation from high schools, colleges and universities add life's beauty and ugliness, and further present intricacies and nuances that multiply life's excitements and challenges. College/university graduation creates job opportunities that have transformational values; and, landing jobs and surviving in jobs create their own joys and frustrations. Interestingly, graduate and professional degrees (e.g., medicine, law, and engineering) tend to develop futuristic value-added attributes that have positive sustainability effects. All these human experiences are culturally interwoven with positive and negative interactions; and they are logically intertwined with socio-cultural intricacies and nuances that impinge upon life's sustainability. In consonance, these experiences can be extremely loaded for African Americans and other CLD and vulnerable persons who add cultural variabilities to already challenging situations (Majors & Billson, 1992).

After all academic attainments and trainings, the next stage is to land a job; and, this again presents more socio-cultural opportunities and challenges that come with life. To be successful on the job, we have to work hard and network with fellow workers. Remember, we do not own the company that employed us; and, even if we own our company, we have to care for our workers or they will leave our company. Every stage of life has myriad socio-cultural steps to deal with in order to be successful (Minton & Schneider, 1980). During all these stages or steps, frustrations can creep in at any time; and, these frustrations can create mental health, family, and other related anti-social problems that are in antipathy to the attainment of success and life's sustainability. Integral to our survival in all the aforementioned stages or steps are multidimensional and multicultural mazes that we must meander through. We must relate to and network with peers, colleagues, teachers, professors, mentors, bosses, supervisors, and the host of others who are different from us. Each person plays a role that affects us, our education, employment, and survival. In all, we inevitably must learn to collaborate, consult, and cooperate with others different from us in our religion, ability, inability, race, culture, skin color, behavior, thinking, intelligence, strength, and weakness, to mention a few. In other words, we must interact with others different from us, despite our multicultural values; and, those who intend to interact with us must make efforts to understand who we are, what inspires us, and what frustrates us. If these efforts are not made, there will be cultural collision and collusion (Beachum & McCray, 2011).

Building Optimism Without False Hopes

It is alright to be very optimistic in whatever we do, especially in our multicultural journeys; but, what is not alright is being overzealous about our hopes and promises. We must shrewdly understand when we have tried our best and when our best is not good enough. This is when spirituality comes to play—when one door closes, another door opens up! The fact remains that nobody is shielded from going through some intricate multidimensional steps; and the journey of life (i.e., our multicultural journey) involves phases and steps that lead to other steps. Each step can be mutually inclusive or exclusive. When one step is blocked, we take another route to get to a new step (Obiakor, 2023a). Cumulatively, these myriad steps are unending and connected to multicultural joys and barriers of life.

Sometimes, when things are going good, we forget our stages or steps; and when they are going bad, we remember the horrendous nature of every step. For example, in William Shakespeare's *Macbeth* (see Walter J. Black, Inc., 1944), the hero, Macbeth forgot some socio-cultural steps and refused to follow the natural steps. He wanted to abide by the predictions of the witches to get to the next step by any means necessary. To move faster, he and his wife killed King Duncan and usurped the Kingly throne. He found himself suffering for not following appropriate socio-cultural steps—he became disappointed by the (a) witches' predictions, (b) death of his wife, and (c) defeat of his soldiers and himself. In the end, he was killed during the war by supporters of the late King Duncan (Obiakor, 2023a). But, looking back, after the death of Macbeth's wife, as most humans, he was frustrated, lamented her loss, made a phenomenal, memorable, and socio-cultural assertion that "life is but a walking shadow." Typically, death is a part of nature—it comes when it comes. In addition, death is loaded with socio-cultural variables (e.g., religion, norms, and values).

A critical analysis of Macbeth's life journeys above reveals a person who failed himself because of his lack of understanding of the socio-cultural stages of life. Though in the end, he acknowledged that "life is but a walking shadow," he exposed this lack of understanding when he (a) disrupted nature's peace and took another person's life, and (b) questioned the timing of his wife's death. It was obvious that he wanted what he wanted despite the time, risk, law, or culture involved. While it was okay for Macbeth to want change, it was iconoclastically against nature and culture to want change drastically and fraudulently. In today's changing world, Macbeth's actions and experiences provide great socio-cultural lessons for all. As we work hard to achieve our goals, we must not be surprised about some failures, imperfections, oppositions, and hateful actions. But, as multicultural beings, we must never give up—our hard work, determination, patience, and vision must be our tools (Obiakor, 2024a, 2024b).

Advancing Life Journeys

Our life journeys are intertwined with our multicultural journeys. To attain real success in our education, job, and life journeys; we must take multicultural steps to survive. No journey worth engaging in is easy! In the end, we must never be too careful, too vigilant, and too spiritual in our multicultural or life journeys (Obiakor, 2001, 2008, 2023a, 2023b). Our eyes must continuously be on the prize! This means that we must:

- Know who we are, including our cultural strengths and weaknesses.
- Be arrogantly humble or humbly arrogant.
- Learn the facts when in doubt or confusion.
- Care about others and treat them as we will like to be treated.
- Respect human differences.
- Value different races, cultures, and languages.
- Never silence any voice, even if it sounds heretical.
- Check the temperature of our surroundings.
- Understand the intricacies of life's stages.
- Work hard to do the right things to be successful in our life's endeavors
- Take advantage of life's opportunities
- Have good moral compass.
- Change our thinking, as needed.
- Build self-concepts by leaving people with good feelings about us.
- Network with others and utilize human resources by collaborating, consulting, and cooperating.
- Make the right choices and shift paradigms and powers, as needed.
- Be aware and careful of what we hear, see, say, and do.
- Fight the "good" fight and not fight the "bad" fight.
- Continue to learn and teach with different techniques.
- Understand that what we put in is what we get. (see Obiakor, 2023a, p. 3)

Conclusion

Life is full of interwoven intricate journeys from the time we are born until when we live this earth. Intertwined with these journeys are multidimensional experiences that require multicultural skill-sets and interactions to maximize potentials, whether in education, employment, and life. As a result, our typical statements of "that's not how I was raised" and "that's not how we do it" seem to be off-the-mark. Clearly, we are all learners who learn differently; and, our life journeys call for efforts to learn new skills and unlearning old habits. We must consider that those involved in these journeys are human beings who are intra-individually and inter-individually different. When we understand this, we begin to work together, learn together, teach together, and enjoy the very essence of collaboration, consultation, and cooperation at all levels. To a large extent, we must also begin to appreciate the wonders of our own individualities and understand that no part of our life journeys is divorced from our multicultural experiences, interactions, and ways of living. These points are critical in building harmony, unity, and love in our schools, colleges/universities, organizations, communities, nation, and world.

Finally, our life journeys are not just theoretical explorations; they are real socio-cultural experiences of real human beings. It is time we started viewing ourselves as unique cultural individuals who are an important part of a collective of people. By doing this, we set the stage for engaging in critical thinking and problem-solving that are rooted in what we see, hear, feel, say, and do. Though many of us seem to have forgotten that we are higher primates who are supposed to think "outside-the-box" and at higher levels, it is our responsibility to think deeper and search for "new" meanings. We have the obligation to infuse into our spaces good quantities of intelligent quotient, quality of life, heart, social quotient, and emotional intelligence. Without such infusion that will inspire us to shift our paradigms and powers, our life journeys will be darker and harder to imagine. In the end, we must see ourselves as multicultural citizens who live in a multicultural world that is loaded with multicultural journeys. And, we must be willing to learn, grow, and teach from our journeys.

AFTERWORD: MULTICULTURALISM AND BEYOND

Carlos R. McCray
Montclair State University

> I place you here! This is the left of the Union line. You understand! You are to hold this ground at all costs! (General Strong Vincent as cited in White, 2023, p. 174)

White's (2023) revelation of General Vincent's statement exposed the imperative nature of building a United States that must be held together at all costs. Holding the nation together is tantamount to valuing the different peoples, cultures, and entities within it. It is in this spirit that Festus E. Obiakor writes this book, *No Time to Retreat: Why We Must Solidify Multicultural Education*. As someone who has written on the needs for schools to implement multicultural education programs, I am disheartened at what is taking place in and out of many schools around the country today. There appears to be a tendency of switching on and off the lights of togetherness and human valuing at the expense of our country's future. For example, when Mr. George Floyd was murdered at the hands of police officers in Minneapolis, Minnesota, our nation, as well as the world, witnessed almost unprecedented protests undergirded by folks from all walks of life. People in the United States, as well as from around the world, were shocked at what they had seen on their television sets that it moved a plethora of them into action. There was an assumption that the protests that were on television sets after George Floyd's murder would result in positive steps and progress. But today, we are seeing retreats and retrenchments at all levels. As Obiakor reiterates in this book, this is "no time to retreat."

There is no doubt that recent retreats and retrenchments are in antipathy to the dedicated efforts by freedom loving, futuristic multiculturalists like Obiakor and others. These pushbacks have become threats to making our society a more just and equitable place for everyone, regardless of race, ethnicity, gender, national origin, or religious preference. We can no longer pretend that our nation is homogeneous and not made up of individuals from different walks of life. Though I have been somewhat discouraged at the levels of pushback on issues such as multiculturalism, Critical Race Theory, Diversity, Equity and Inclusion (DEI), I feel energized by Obiakor's *No Time to Retreat*. I am reminded of Dr. Martin Luther King, Jr.'s February 10, 1961 speech that he delivered at New York University. As Dr. King (1961) noted, progress is not always linear and "human progress is neither automatic nor inevitable. Every step toward the goal of justice requires sacrifice, suffering, and struggle…" This quote should give us a sense of hope and reassurance that "the arch of the moral universe is long, but it bends toward justice." In consonance, former President Obama (2016) indicated in his commencement address at Rutgers University that it takes all of us to ensure that it bends toward justice. Referring to Dr. King's quote, President Obama (2016) remarked,

> I believe that. But I also believe that the arc of our nation, the arc of our world, does not bend toward justice, or freedom, or equality, or prosperity on its own. It depends on us, on the choices we make, particularly at certain inflection points in history…

And, this is certainly an inflection point in our nation's history regarding all of us deciding what type of country we want for ourselves, as well as our posterity. This is why Obiakor's book, *No Time to Retreat*, is so poignant and timely. Obiakor realizes that we are facing a critical moment when civil rights and liberties are taken for granted. And, to ensure that the momentum we have gained throughout the years continues, we must be willing to take a stand and not yield any ground on the ideals and values that are so dear to us.

So, what are those values that we hold so dear to us that are now under assault? The very essence of multiculturalism is the notion of respecting and valuing the diversity that is found within our society. This is the absolute base line of what multiculturalism entails. When there is an attack on program initiatives such as DEI, such attacks are tantamount to attacks on multiculturalism. After all, the origins of multiculturalism were centered on the exact concepts of DEI. Thus, attacks on DEI are very similar to attacks that were levied on multicultural education back in the 1980s and 1990s. As it appears today, I must admit that attacks on DEI are so orchestrated that they make attacks on multiculturalism to look trivial. And, it is critical that we make this connectivity, as seen below.

Diversity

As indicated earlier, one of the hallmarks of multiculturalism is that it seeks to promote a better understanding of the diversity that is found within our schools and society. McCray and Beachum (2014) argued that "the lack of diverse content being offered to an increasingly diverse student population was the ultimate catalyst for what is today called multicultural education" (p. 23). As McCray and Beachum (2014) indicated, "…the basic premise of multiculturalism entails an approach that promotes cultural pluralism by ensuring that all students regardless of their race, gender, sexual orientation, mental and physical ability, socioeconomic status, and religion have an equal opportunity to learn in school by changing the total educational environment" (pp. 23–24). This definition of multiculturalism is what undergirds the promotion of diversity within our schools. As our nation continues to become more diverse, it is crucial that school leaders make concerted efforts in ensuring that the school curriculum has embedded within it the principles of multiculturalism. One principle that has been promoted by Banks (2001) that is also connected to increasing diversity is the concept of *prejudice reduction*. In 1954—the year in which the Supreme Court made its ruling in *Brown v. Board of Education* case, G. W. Allport established his theory, the contact hypothesis. This contact hypothesis meant that the more contact people from different groups have with one another, the more likely there is a reduction of prejudice. Allport's (1954) contact hypothesis closely aligns with Banks's (2001) prejudice reduction premise. In essence, prejudice reduction calls on school leaders to cultivate "an environment where intolerance and bigotry have been removed from the school culture" (McCray et al., 2021, p. 69). When the notion of promoting diversity is jettisoned out of the educative process, there is the realistic consequence of losing gains that have been made throughout the years in reducing prejudice and biases that many individuals sometimes bring with them to schools and classrooms.

It is important to note that an assault on diversity has the potential to reinforce *groupthink*. *Groupthink* is where individuals within an organization share similar background, thus leading to similar worldviews and insights (Kowert, 2002). Such thinking has the tendency to stifle an organization's growth and prohibit it from seeing potential blind spots (see Kowert, 2002). Likewise, groupthink can have a drastic impact in the field of education and related fields. One could argue that the consequences of groupthink in the field of education are more drastic than in the field of industry. When groupthink occurs within the corporate world, the outcomes are a reduction in the bottom line and profits, sometimes at the expense of workers well-being. And, when groupthink occurs in education, it is undergirded by *deficit thinking* and the consequences can be devastating to an entire group of students within our schools. McCray et al. (2021) reaffirmed that "deficit thinking is where some school administrators and educators' default position toward students of color is one of intellectual inferiority" (p. 69). Thus, one can easily connect the dots here and understand why Obiakor, in this book, admonishes those who care about a socially just society to not retreat in this time of uncertainty.

If diversity, which is a major underpinning of multiculturalism, is undermined within our schools, there is the strong potential that many of our schools could see a rise in prejudice and bias incidents. In addition, there is a strong possibility that many more decisions and policies will be implemented by homogenous groups, where groupthink plays a role. Only time would tell as to just how devastating such results could be for groups that have historically been targeted because of their race, ethnicity, gender, religion, and national origin. In this book, Obiakor urges us to be vigilant and do whatever we can to solidify multicultural education.

Equity

The concept of equity is very much embedded within the notion of multiculturalism. In one of Banks's (2001) five dimensions of multiculturalism, he put forth the notion, *equity pedagogy*. Of course, the concept of equity has a broader application in society. In fact, one could make the argument that no other social justice term has been made to be more divisive in the United States than the notion of equity. In its simplest form, the notion of equity means being fair and just by providing what people need to be successful in life. Equity differs from equality in one major way: the notion of equality entails treating everyone in society the same. It does not consider the fact that some groups have been historically marginalized. Whereas equity does take into consideration that some groups in society, who have been relegated to second or third class citizens, might need more resources to thrive and beyond. Equity has also come under attack at various educational levels. When some individuals demonize DEI within our schools, equity is being demonized alongside multiculturalism. It is important to have a clear understanding of the role that DEI is playing within the field of education. It is now imperative for scholars whose work is grounded within social justice to take a stand by articulating just how critical it is for educators and institutions to continue to promote DEI and multiculturalism within the school and classrooms.

Clearly, the threat to remove equity from our schools and classrooms jeopardizes Banks' (2001) notion of equity pedagogy. Earlier McGee Banks and Banks (1995) defined

> equity pedagogy as teaching strategies and classroom environments that help students from diverse racial, ethnic, and cultural groups attain the knowledge, skills and attitudes needed to function effectively within, and help create and perpetuate, a just, humane, and democratic society. (p. 152)

In the same dimension, McCray et al. (2010) added that equity pedagogy is a "process that allows teachers to use different teaching methods and styles that tend to correlate with students of diverse cultural and social backgrounds" (p. 39). Here, we see that the notion of equity when conflated with teaching and learning within the classroom is fundamental in reaching students from diverse backgrounds and ensuring that a high level of learning for ALL students is indeed taking place. And "if critical [equity] pedagogy is going to be a part of the educational classroom, educators have to make an effort to validate...experiences that students bring with them to the classroom from their respective communities" (McCray et al., 2010, p. 39). When school leaders and educators acquiesce to the noise and rhetoric from those who wish to score political points by attacking DEI, they are in essence putting in jeopardy historically marginalized students who can benefit greatly from instruction that considers their lived experiences. And more importantly, when school leaders and educators become dismissive of infusing equity pedagogy within the classroom, they are also perhaps producing learners who are ill-equipped to critique the "hegemonic" practices within the classroom and broader society (McGee Banks & Banks, 1995). In this book, Obiakor emphasizes these points in more ways than one.

Equity pedagogy takes into consideration how educators teach and what is being taught in relation to the array of diversity that is found within the classroom. But as mentioned, it is also focused on giving students the tools needed to make socially just improvements to their communities and society. It should come as no surprise that there are those who would wish to see the concept of equity be thrown out of the educative process all together. Thus, the hands of school leaders and educators would essentially be tied in using their professional understanding and judgment as to what and how to teach. McGee Banks and Banks (1995) emphasized that equity pedagogy demands that students be given the tools to critique and question the knowledge that is being presented to them. Such critiques prepare students to inevitably question other arrangements within our society. As McGee Banks and Banks (1995) concluded, "helping students to become reflective and active citizens of a democratic society is at the essence of our conception of equity pedagogy" (p. 152). In this book, Obiakor explains these points in a poignant fashion.

Inclusion

When individuals look to score political points or take us back to a time in which our society was not a fair and equal society for all by attacking DEI, they are also attacking the notion of an inclusive society. The "I" in DEI represents inclusion. And, logic would dictate that if you are an opponent of DEI, then you are in essence an opponent of inclusion. There is plethora of ways in which an analysis could be applied to the attack on ensuring our society and organizations are inclusive for individuals from all walks of life. In a related fashion, Banks's (2001) dimension of multiculturalism connects nicely with inclusion within our schools by empowering the school culture. In consonance, McCray and Beachum (2014) found that "the idea of empowering the school culture entails school leaders and educators creating a school climate that instills in… [diverse] learners a sense of acceptance and belonging" (p. 15). Logically, the notion of acceptance and belonging represents inclusion at the highest level.

Remarkably, Obiakor, in this book, focuses on human valuing and inclusion. It is clear that people do not get involved with people who they do not like. They like to exclude such people in their activities and do not care if exclusion prevents them from growing as valuable human beings. In essence, people nurture and develop what they care about and throw away what they do not care about. Logically, when we include people, we develop and empower them to be the best that they can be. McCray and Beachum (2014) supported the notion of self-development because it enhances "the sense of self-realization and self-assertion among [diverse] learners" (p. 18). Inclusiveness empowers the school culture, self-assertion, and self-preparedness. For example, many African American students bring with them to school an enormous amount of what Yosso (2005) called *aspiration capital*. It is the aspirational capital that gives students the belief that if they try hard, they will achieve academic success, as well as success in life. This thinking encourages human development and self-enhancement. Educators and related professionals must be focused on how to prepare all learners, especially vulnerable learners, for inclusive communities and society. Relatedly, when these learners feel that they are not valued within their schools, it can have a devastating impact on their sense of self-aspiration, which is a major component of the pedagogy of self-development. I agree with Obiakor, in this book, that exclusion has multidimensional negative impacts and consequences on students, families, schools, colleges/universities, institutions, organizations, and communities.

Moving Forward

DEI and critical race theory have been made by some in our society to be the boogey man of the 21st century. But, they are not! Obiakor, in this book, demonstrates that multiculturalism is here to stay and that our future as a society depends on human and cultural valuing. We need people who care! We need programs that can move our society forward! And, we all must ensure that we live in a society that is undergirded by DEI! Obiakor emphasizes these critical points, especially because of their connectivity to general and special education, human valuing, and social justice. I agree with Obiakor that these multicultural issues can no longer be swept under the rug.

Thinking about the book, *No Time to Retreat*, two great historical figures, Dr. Martin Luther King, Jr. and President Ulysses S. Grant come to mind. Dr. King (1961) fervently believed justice would ultimately prevail in our society. When Dr. King (1961) noted that "the arch of the moral universe is long, but it bends toward justice," he knew that for justice to prevail in our society, we had to do the necessary work...it was simply not going to happen on its own. He was a man of courage and conviction who paid the ultimate sacrifice for what he believed in. Likewise, President Grant was also a man of bravery and principle; and, it was put on full display throughout the Civil War. When General Grant initiated the Sherman campaign, this was his way of not conceding any ground to Lee's army. General Grant went on the offensive! Both Dr. King and President Grant showed remarkable leadership in moving the United States forward and not allowing it to be overcome with racial oppression.

As I reflect on the future, there was another Civil War hero, Colonel Joshua Lawerence Chamberlain who oversaw the Twentieth Maine regiment. Many historians have indicated that his actions at Gettysburg on that hot July day in 1863 were pivotal in helping the Union army to defeat the Confederates at the battle of Gettysburg (White, 2023). Prior to the battle on Little Round Top at Gettysburg, Col. Chamberlain had been told by his commanding officer, General Vincent, that his army must not give ground or retreat under any circumstances. General Vincent told Col. Chamberlain that "I place you here! This is the left of the Union line. You understand! You are to hold this ground at all cost" (White, 2023, p. 174)! Col. Chamberlain knew that if the Twentieth Maine retreated, Law's Brigade, which consisted of the 15th Alabama, could sweep around the left flank and perhaps win the battle, which would place the Union army in a precarious position (White, 2023). As students of history know, especially if they have watched the movie "Gettysburg," Col Chamberlain did not retreat on that faithful day. He did not give ground; and, his actions probably helped the Union Army to give Robert E. Lee's army its first major defeat of the war. The battle at Gettysburg changed the entire trajectory of the war for the Union. I am hoping that *No Time to Retreat* will be a transformational book that would help us to learn so much about the imperative nature of multicultural education in our nation and world. We must value ourselves, our communities, and our humanity! Without such human valuing, we are destined to fail as a nation of different peoples.

Conclusion

In this book, Obiakor reminds us to value our intra-individual and inter individual differences and our general humanity. We must be dedicated, resilient, and forward-looking in our mission and vision; and, our goals and objectives must be clear. We want to leave the world better than we saw it; but, we cannot accomplish this overall goal, if we fail our children and youth. Sending them to jail should not be our best option—we want to save our children and youth from the iniquities of the past. For those of us in this country who are committed to social justice within our schools, organizations, and society, we must—now more than ever—draw on the examples that have been provided to us by such historical figures. For example, Dr. Martin Luther King, Jr. fought against Jim Crow (i.e., segregation) and the right for all African Americans to vote without intimidation. In essence, he fought to make this country a more socially just place to live for all Americans. Col. Chamberlain did his fighting on the battlefield. Though he also seriously considered becoming a minister, he chose to become a professor until he volunteered to serve in the Union army (White, 2023). And, Gen. Grant did his fighting on the Battlefield, as well as in the Oval Office as our 18th President. His dedication and commitment to the maxim, "No Time to Retreat" was needed to destroy Lee's army. And, after leaving the army and becoming President, he continued to fight to ensure that freedmen and women in the South were able to vote without intimidation. Further, he was relentless in fighting the Ku Klux Klan (Chernow, 2017). In this book, Obiakor similarly shows that he wants us to be dedicated and committed to DEI and multicultural principles and challenges us to be the best we can be. I agree with Obiakor that this is *No Time to Retreat*. We cannot allow concepts such DEI or multiculturalism to be taken over by simplistic and close-minded utterances and campaigns. Certainly, we do not want to become the generation that surrendered its voice only later to realize that multiculturalism, diversity, equity, and inclusion have been instrumental in moving our nation toward a more perfect union.

References

Allport, G. W. (1954). *The nature of prejudice*. Addison-Wesley.
Banks, J. A. (2001). Multicultural education: Characteristics and goals. In J. A. Banks & C. H. McGee-Banks (Eds.), *Multicultural education: Issues and perspectives* (4th ed., pp. 3–30). John Wiley & Sons.
Chernow, R. (2017). *Grant*. Penguin Books.
Kowert, P. A. (2002). *Groupthink or deadlock: When do leaders learn from their advisor*. SUNY Press.
McCray, C. R., & Beachum, F. D. (2014). *School leadership in a diverse society: Helping school prepare all students for success*. Information Age Publishing.
McCray, C. R., Beachum, F. D., & Reggio, P. F. (2021). *School leadership in a diverse society: Helping school prepare all students for success*. Information Age Publishing.
McCray, C. R., Grant, C., & Beachum, F. D. (2010). Pedagogy of self-development: The role the black church can have on African American students. *The Journal of Negro Education, 79*(3), 233–248.

McGee Banks, C. A., & Banks, J. A. (1995). Equity pedagogy: An essential component of multicultural education. *Theory into Practice, 34*(3), 152–158.

White, R. C. (2023). *On great fields: The life and unlikely heroism of Joshua Lawerence Chamberlain.* Penguin Random House LLC.

Yosso, T. J. (2005). Whose culture has capital? A critical race theory discussion of community cultural wealth. *Race, Ethnicity and Education, 8,* 69–91.

REFERENCES

Allport, G. W. (1954). *The nature of prejudice.* Addison-Wesley.
Arllen, N., Cheney, D., & Warger, C. (1997). Recapturing the promise of a future imperiled: Ways to make community-based collaboration work. In L. Bullock & R. Gable (Eds.), *Making collaboration work for children, youth, families, schools, and community* (pp. 39–43). Council for Exceptional Children.
Banks, J. A. (1998). The lives and values of researchers: Implications for educating citizens in a multicultural society. *Educational Researcher, 27*(7), 4–17.
Banks, J. A. (2001). Multicultural education: Characteristics and goals. In J. A. Banks & C. H. McGee-Banks (Eds.), *Multicultural education: Issues and perspectives* (4th ed., pp. 3–30). John Wiley & Sons.
Barnlund, D. C. (1976). The mystification of meaning: Doctor-patient encounters. *Journal of Medical Education, 51,* 716–725.
Baron, R. A., & Byrne, D. (1994). *Social psychology: Understanding human interactions* (7th ed.). Allyn & Bacon.
Beachum, F. D. (2023). Afterword: Everyone hates hate. In F. E. Obiakor (Ed.), *Reducing hate through multicultural education and transformation* (pp. 89–100). Information Age.
Beachum, F. D., & McCray, C. R. (2011). *Cultural collision and collusion: Reflections on hip-hop culture, values, and schools.* Peter Lang.
Beam, G. C. (1980). *A kindergarten/primary program for culturally different potentially gifted students in an inner city school in Albuquerque, New Mexico.* Final Report. Albuquerque Special Preschool.
Bertram, T., & Pascal, C. (2002). What counts in early learning. In O. N. Saracho & B. Spodek (Eds.), *Contemporary perspectives in early childhood curriculum* (pp. 241–256). Information Age.
Biden, J. (2021, June 25). *Executive orders on diversity, equity, inclusion, and accessibility.* White House.
Block, N. J., & Dworkin, G. (1976). *The IQ controversy: Critical readings.* Pantheon Books.
Bronoski, J. (1971). *The identity of man.* American Museum Science Books.
Bruni, F. (2024). *The age of grievance.* Avid Reader Press/Simon & Schuster.
Campt, T. M. (2023). *A Black gaze: Artists changing how we see.* Penguin USA.
Carroll, R. (2021). *Surviving the White gaze: A memoir.* Simon & Schuster.

Chandler, D. (1998). Notes on "the gaze". http://aber.ac.uk/media/documents/gaze//gaze.html

Chernow, R. (2017). *Grant*. Penguin Books.

Cochran, E. P., & Cotayo, A. (1983). *Louis D. Brandeis High School demonstration bilingual enrichment college preparatory program*. New York City Public Schools.

Covey, S. R. (1990). *The 7 habits of highly effective people: Powerful lessons in personal change*. A Fireside Book.

Dannenberg, A. C. (1984). Issues in education for the gifted. In A. H. Passow (Ed.), *The gifted and the talented: Their education and development*. University of Chicago Press.

Da Ros-Voseles, D., & Sally Fowler-Haughey, S. (2007, September). Why children's dispositions should matter to all teachers. *Beyond the Journal: Young Children on the Web*, 1–7.

Dewey, J. (1958). *Philosophy of education*. Littlefield, Adams.

Dewey, J. (1960). *On experience, nature, and freedom*. Bobbs-Merrill.

Diangelo, R. (2022). *Nice racism: How progressive White people perpetuate racial harm*. Beacon Press.

Donnelly, C. (2024). Leadership green flags. https://chris-donnelly.co.uk/

Dooley, E. A., & Toscano-Nixon, C. M. (2002). Community involvement in education. In F. E. Obiakor, P. A. Grant, & E. A. Dooley (Eds.), *Educating all learners: Refocusing the comprehensive support model* (pp. 90–112). Charles C. Thomas Publisher.

Dukach, D. (2022, January–February). DEI gets real. *Harvard Business Review*, 1–6.

Dunn, L. (2020, November 6). What is diversity, equity, and inclusion? http://inclusionhub.com

Every student succeeds act of 2015, Pub. L. 114-95 (2015).

Fabris, M. E. (1992). Using multimedia in the multicultural classroom. *Journal of Educational Technology Systems, 21*, 163–171.

Ford, B. A. (1995). African American community involvement processes and special education: Essential networks for effective education. In B. A. Ford, F. E. Obiakor, & J. M. Patton (Eds.), *Effective education of African American exceptional learners: New perspectives* (pp. 235–272). Pro-Ed.

Ford, B. A. (2002). African American community resources: Essential educational enhancers for African American children and youth. In F. E. Obiakor & B. A. Ford (Eds), *Creating successful learning environments for African American learners with exceptionalities* (pp. 159–173). Corwim Press.

Ford, B. A., Obiakor, F. E., & Patton, J. M. (1995). *Effective education of African American exceptional learners: New perspectives*. Pro-Ed.

Ford, B. A., Vakil, S., & Kline, L. S. (2019). School-community partnerships: Educating young children. In F. E. Obiakor, T. Banks, J. Graves, & A. F. Rotatori (Eds.), *Educating young children with and without exceptionalities: New perspectives* (pp. 91–104). Information Age.

Ford, D. Y., & Harris, J. J. (1999). *Multicultural gifted education*. Teachers College Press.

Frankl, V. E. (1984). *Man's search for meaning: An introduction to logotherapy* (3rd ed.). Touchstone Book.

Freehill, M. F. (1974, Winter). Intelligence, empathy and methodological bias about teaching the gifted. *Gifted Child Quarterly*, 247–248.

Freire, P. (1996). *Pedagogy of the oppressed*. Continuum Publishing.

Friedman, T. L. (2005). *The world is flat: A brief history of the twenty-first century*. Farrar, Straus, and Giroux.

Fulghum, R. (1990). *All I really need to know I learned in kindergarten: Uncommon thoughts on common things*. Villard Books.

Gardner, H. (1993). *Multiple intelligences: The theory in practice*. Basic Books.

Goleman, D. (1995). *Emotional intelligence: Why it can matter more than IQ*. Bantam Books.

Gordon, T. (1975). *PET: Parent effectiveness training*. Plume Book.

Gorski, P. C. (2001). *Multicultural education and the internet: Intersections and integration*. McGraw-Hill.

Gould, S. J. (1981). *The mismeasure of man*. W. W. Norton.

Grennon Brooks, J., & Brooks, M. G. (2001). *In search of understanding: The case for constructivist classrooms*. Merrill Prentice Hall.

Greyman, L. (2025). *The Minds Journal*. https://themindsjournal.com

Gutek, G. L. (2006). *American education in a global society: International and comparative perspectives* (2nd ed.). Waveland Press.

Hansford, S. J. (1985, October). What it takes to be a g/t teacher. *Gifted Child Monthly*, 15–17.

Howell, D., Norris, A., & Willimas, K. L. (2019). Towards Black gaze theory: How Black female teachers make Black students visible. *Urban Education Policy and Research Annals, 6*(1), 20–30.

Individuals with disabilities education improvement act of 2004, Pub. L. 108-446 (2004).

Jonassen, D. H., Howland, J. L., Moore, J. L., & Marra, R. M. (2003). *Learning to solve problems and technology: A constructivist perspective* (2nd ed.). Merrill/Prentice Hall.

Kaplan, S. (2005). Layering differentiated curricula for the gifted and talented. In F. A. Karnes & S. M. Bean (Eds.), *Methods and materials for teaching the gifted* (2nd ed., pp. 107–132). Prufrock.

Katz, L. G., & Raths, J. (1985). Dispositions as goals for education. *Teaching and Teacher Education, 1*(4), 301–307.

Katz, L. G., & Raths, J. (1986, July). Dispositional goals for teacher education: Problems of identification and assessment. Paper presented at the World Assembly of the International Council on Education for Teaching, Kingston, Jamaica.

King, M. L. (1961, February 10). *The future of Integration*. Speech audio recording. YouTube. https://www.youtube.com/watch?v=QAKR_5JzZaA

Kowert, P. A. (2002). *Groupthink or deadlock: When do leaders learn from their advisor*. SUNY Press.

Kroth, R. L., & Edge, D. (1997). *Strategies for communicating with parents and families of exceptional children* (3rd ed.). Love Publishing.

Lincoln, A. (1858, September 2). *Lincoln v. Douglas debate*. Clinton, IL.

Maccini, P., Gagnon, J. C., & Hughes, C. A. (2002). Technology-based practices for secondary students with learning disabilities. *Learning Disability Quarterly, 25*, 247–261.

MacDonald, H. (2024). Disparate impact thinking is destroying our civilization. *Imprimis, 53*(2), 1–7.

Majors, R., & Billson, J. M. (1992). *Cool pose: The dilemmas of Black manhood in America*. Lexington Books.

Martin, P., & Widgren, J. (2002). *International migration: Facing the challenge.* Population Reference Bureau.

McCray, C. R., & Beachum, F. D. (2014). *School leadership in a diverse society: Helping schools prepare all students for success.* Information Age.

McCray, C. R., Beachum, F. D., & Reggio, P. F. (2021). *School leadership in a diverse society: Helping schools prepare all students for success* (3rd ed.). Information Age.

McCray, C. R., Grant, C., & Beachum, F. D. (2010). Pedagogy of self-development: The role the black church can have on African American students. *Journal of Negro Education, 79*(3), 233–248.

McGee Banks, C. A., & Banks, J. A. (1995). Equity pedagogy: An essential component of multicultural education. *Theory into Practice, 34*(3), 152–158.

Minton, H. L., & Schneider, F. W. (1980). *Differential psychology.* Waveland Press.

Obama, B. H. (2016, May 15). *Rutgers university commencement address.* Speech audio recording. YouTube. http://www.youtube.com/watch?v=kCABjFT32A

Obiakor, F. E. (2001). *It even happens in "good" schools: Responding to cultural diversity in today's classrooms.* Corwin Press.

Obiakor, F. E. (2007). *Multicultural special education: Culturally responsive teaching.* Pearson Merrill/Prentice Hall.

Obiakor, F. E. (2008). *The eight-step approach to multicultural learning and teaching* (3rd ed.). Kendall/Hunt.

Obiakor, F. E. (2014). Afterword: Leadership for diversity. In C. R. McCray & F. D. Beachum (Eds.), *School leadership in a diverse society: Helping schools prepare all students for success* (pp. 123–126). Information Age.

Obiakor, F. E. (2018). *Powerful multicultural essays for innovative educators and leaders: Optimizing "hearty" conversations.* Information Age.

Obiakor, F. E. (2020). *Valuing other voices: Discourses that matter in education, social justice, and multiculturalism.* Information Age.

Obiakor, F. E. (2021). *Multiculturalism still matters in education and society: Responding to changing times.* Information Age.

Obiakor, F. E. (2023a, August). Beyond phase 1: Advancing our academic, employment, and life journeys. Invited presentation at the Obodoukwu General Assembly (OGA), Washington, DC.

Obiakor, F. E. (2023b). *Reducing hate through multicultural education and transformation.* Information Age.

Obiakor, F. E. (2024a, March). Executive editor's comments: Dispositions that foster multicultural dispositions. *Multicultural Learning and Teaching, 19*(1), 1–6.

Obiakor, F. E. (2024b, March). What the mouth says matters to multicultural learners in general and special education. *Multicultural Learning and Teaching, 19*(1), 23–31.

Obiakor, F. E., & Algozzine, B. (1995). *Managing problem behaviors: Perspectives for general and special educators.* Kendall/Hunt.

Obiakor, F. E., Aluka, I. J., Obiakor, G. C., & Obi, S. O. (2024, March). Educating culturally and linguistically diverse students with disabilities in inclusive settings: Beyond debates. *Multicultural Learning and Teaching, 19*(1), 111–122.

Obiakor, F. E., Banks, T., Graves, J., & Rotatori, A. F. (2019). *Educating young children with and without exceptionalities: New perspectives.* Information Age.

Obiakor, F. E., Banks, T., Rotatori, A. F., & Utley, C. (2017). *Leadership matters in the education of students with special needs in the 21st century.* Information Age.

Obiakor, F. E., & Ford, B. A. (2002). *Creating successful learning environments for African American learners with exceptionalities.* Corwin Press.

Obiakor, F. E., Grant, P. A., & Dooley, E. A. (2002). *Educating all learners: Refocusing the comprehensive support model.* Charles C. Thomas Publisher.

Obiakor, F. E., Grant, P. A., & Obi, S. O. (2010). *Voices of foreign-born African American teacher educators in the United States.* Nova Science Publishers.

Obiakor, F. E., Mehring, T. A., & Schwenn, J. O. (1997). *Disruption, disaster, and death: Helping students deal with crises.* The Council for Exceptional Children.

Palmer, P. J. (1998). *The courage to teach: Exploring the inner landscape of a teacher's life.* Jossey Bass Publishers.

Pope, A. (1711). *An essay on criticism. Pitt Press Series.* Cambridge University Press.

Rabelo, V. C., Robotham, K. J., & McCluney, C. L. (2021). "Against a sharp white background": How Black women experience the white gaze at work. *Gender, Work and Organization, 28*(5), 1840–1858.

Roche, T. (2025, February 14). *Letter re-stating our commitment to academic independence and global participation.* Emerald Publishing Limited.

Sassen, S. (1998). *Globalization and its discontents: Essays on the new mobility of people and money.* The New Press.

Schlesinger, A. Jr. (1999). What is an American? In S. Heckney (Ed.), *One America indivisible: A national conversation on American pluralism and identity.* National Endowment for the Humanities.

Stimson, C. (2024, March). Rogue prosecutors and the rise of crime. *Imprimis, 53*(3), 1–5.

Swindoll, C. (2012). Attitude. http://thelittlerebellion.com

Thomas Nelson, Inc. (1994). Holy Bible: King James version.

Tomlinson, C. A. (1999). *The differentiated classroom: Responding to the needs of all learners.* The Association for Supervision and Curriculum Development.

Tomlinson, C. A. (2005). *How to differentiate instruction in mixed ability classrooms* (2nd ed.). Pearson.

Tomlinson, C. A. (2011). Fulfilling the promise of differentiation. http://www.carltomlinson.com

Trump, D. J. (2020, September 22). *Executive order on combating race and sex stereotyping.* White House.

Trump, D. J. (2025a, January 20). *Ending radical and wasteful government DEI programs and preferencing.* White House.

Trump, D. J. (2025b, January 21). *Executive order: Ending illegal discrimination and restoring merit-based opportunity.* White House.

Tye, K. A. (1991). *Global education: From thought to action.* Association for Supervision and Curriculum Development.

United Nations. (2024, March). *World happiness report 2024.*

Urwin, M. (2024, March 21). Diversity, equity, and inclusion (DEI) in the workplace. https://builtin.com

Villanuena, C. L. (1999). *New technologies for a learning society: Information Technology in educational innovation for development.* UNESCO Asia-Pacific Bureau of Education.

Waldman, P., & Schaller, T. (2024). *White rural rage: The threat to democracy.* Random House.

Walker, S. (2023, December 19). Florida school board approves resolution calling for Bridget Ziegler to resign over Republican sex scandal. *USA Today Network.* http://www.usatoday.com/story/news/nation/2023/12/13

Walter J. Black, Inc. (1944). *The works of William Shakespeare.* Black's Readers Service.

Washington, E. F. (2022a). *The necessary journey: Making real progress on equity and inclusion.* Harvard Business Review Press.

Washington, E. F. (2022b, November-December). The five stages of DEI maturity. *Harvard Business Review,* 1–17.

Werklabs. (2022, March). *What drives a diverse extended workforce: Fostering feelings of inclusion for diverse contingent talent.*

White, R. C. (2023). *On great fields: The life and unlikely heroism of Joshua Lawerence Chamberlain.* Penguin Random House LLC.

Wilmes, D. J. (1988). *Parenting for prevention: For parents, teachers and concerned adults.* Johnson Institute Books.

Yancy, G. (2017). *Black bodies, White gazes: The continuing significance of race* (2nd ed.). Rowman & Littlefield.

Yosso, T. J. (2005). Whose culture has capital? A critical race theory discussion of community cultural wealth. *Race, Ethnicity and Education, 8,* 69–91.

www.ingramcontent.com/pod-product-compliance
Lightning Source LLC
Chambersburg PA
CBHW052134010526
44113CB00036B/2197